PS
3566
.E78
Z474
1999

NNR

Chicago Public Library

R0128972735

Tales of the heart : dreams and mem

JUN 0 2 1999

CHICAGO PUBLIC LIBRARY
NEAR NORTH BRANCH
310 W. DIVISION
CHICAGO, IL 60610

Tales of the Heart

BOOKS BY HARRY MARK PETRAKIS

NOVELS

Lion at My Heart
The Odyssey of Kostas Volakis
A Dream of Kings
In the Land of Morning
The Hour of the Bell
Nick the Greek
Days of Vengeance
Ghost of the Sun

SHORT STORIES

Pericles on 31st Street
The Waves of Night
A Petrakis Reader
Collected Stories

MEMOIRS AND ESSAYS

Stelmark
Reflections: A Writer's Life—A Writer's Work
Tales of the Heart

BIOGRAPHIES

The Founder's Touch
Henry Crown: The Life and Times of the Colonel

HARRY
MARK
PETRAKIS

Tales of the Heart

DREAMS
AND MEMORIES
OF A LIFETIME

Ivan R Dee

CHICAGO 1999

TALES OF THE HEART. Copyright © 1999 by Harry Mark Petrakis. All rights reserved, including the right to reproduce this book or portions thereof in any form. For information, address: Ivan R. Dee, Publisher, 1332 North Halsted Street, Chicago 60622. Manufactured in the United States of America and printed on acid-free paper.

The essays in this book originally appeared in the *Chicago Tribune*, *Chicago Sun-Times*, *Today's Health*, *Ford Times*, *The Rotarian*, *Country Beautiful*, *Chicago Magazine*, *Land's End*, and the *Hellenic Journal*. Their permission to reprint is gratefully acknowledged.

Library of Congress Cataloging-in-Publication Data:
Petrakis, Harry Mark.
    Tales of the heart: dreams and memories of a lifetime / Harry
Mark Petrakis.
        p.   cm.
    ISBN 1-56663-243-9 (alk. paper)
    1. Patrakis, Harry Mark.   2. Authors, American—20th century—
Biography.   3. Authors, American—20th century—Family
relationships.   4. Voyages and travels.   I. Title.
PS3566.E78Z474   1999
813'.54—dc21
    [B]   98-49501

For my dearest Diana,

fifty and three years as sweetheart,

wife, companion, and

maker of superb baklava

CHICAGO PUBLIC LIBRARY
NEAR NORTH BRANCH
310 W. DIVISION
CHICAGO, IL 60610

Contents

Preface

In the classes where I have been teaching writing for many years, I have frequently been asked the difference between an essay and a short story. The customary response would be that the difference is one of focus and transition. In a short story one utilizes imagination and creates a world that might have been. In the essay one begins with a core of fact and creates a world that is. But the truth is that for me the difference barely exists. As far as I am concerned the essay is simply another way of telling a story.

In my childhood I had an old Uncle who would visit us in the small rustic cottage where we spent the summers. We would sit on the screen porch at night, darkness all around us except for the oil lamps flickering shadows across the mesh of the screens where tiny moths flailed their wings in an effort to get through to the flame. Within this haunted setting of lamplight, shadows and flailing moths, my uncle told us stories.

I could never be certain nor did I care whether he was telling us the truth or spinning a fantasy. What was important was that he conjured up for us a life more real, for a little while, than the life we were living.

I think my wonder and delight in storytelling was born then, a wonder and delight I feel to this day.

H. M. P.

Dune Acres, Indiana

Tales of the Heart

◄ FAMILY ►

Ellis Island Memory

I HOLD a browned photograph of my parents and four of my older brothers and sisters taken shortly before they emigrated to America from the island of Crete in 1916. In the seventy years that have passed since then, the countenances in the portrait have remained suspended in time. I inherited the photograph from one of my brothers, and it has hung in the houses where I have lived. Each time I look at it I am reminded that all of life is a mystery that lies not as much in the end as in the beginning.

In the portrait my patriarchal father is seated in an armchair, his family clustered beside him. He wears the ankle-length black cassock and high black stovepipe hat which were the raiment of Greek Orthodox priests in that period. His black hair flows into a black, bushy beard. His eyes are unwavering and vigilant, as if he understands he is the guardian of his flock. Suspended from a chain around his neck hangs the golden cross I saw him wearing for the last time in his coffin thirty-five years later.

My mother, short and small, stands close beside him. She was then in her early twenties, and her eyes and face radiate a serenity and sweetness. I was born in 1923, and another sister, Irene, was born in 1924. As I remember my mother from my childhood, hardship and suffering had carved lines and shadows in her cheeks and about her lips. I can never recall her eyes as tranquil as they appear in the photo.

Dan, my brother, was the oldest of the children. His hair is cropped short and razor-cut above his ears. He wears a white shirt and an oversized tie that dangles so far below his belt and pants it seems part of a clown's apparel. He has the bright, curious stare of a youth surveying new wonders.

Beside him, perhaps perched on a box or chair because she's a head taller than Dan, is my sister Barbara. Her abundant hair frames her extraordinarily large and lucent eyes. The curls falling across her shoulders look fair, although I remember her hair darker later on. Above her head, a large white ribbon billows like a wind-blown sail.

The remaining two children, my sister Tasula and my brother Manuel, appear much younger and smaller although they are separated from the other children by only a few years. Manuel has hair as curly and long as Tasula. She wears a white frock, he a white sailor suit. Both wear white button shoes and white ankle-length socks. But it is their eyes, innocent and comely, that resemble one another as if they were twins.

When the photograph was taken in Crete, they were on the eve of their voyage across the ocean to America. My father had been offered a community in Price, Utah, comprised of young immigrant Cretan coal miners. They had built a church and required a priest. My father could provide them a link to the families and church they had left in

Greece, but he and my mother suffered over the decision whether to leave Crete. Their greatest fears were for their children. Yet it was because of the children, and particularly the educational opportunities they felt America would provide for them, that they made the decision for the journey.

My family posed for the final photograph, leaving it as a keepsake for parents, siblings and friends they were leaving. Afterwards they traveled from Crete to Piraeus, the port of Athens, and boarded a ship for America. Although the conditions and the duration of the crossings had improved over those journeys made in the earlier part of the century, there were still hardships. The children developed a form of ship's fever and Dan suffered from a severe dysentery. There were several frightening lifeboat alerts when German U-boats were detected watching them. (A week before their departure, a U-boat had fired on and damaged an American freighter.) They also endured a fierce storm that rocked their ship with huge waves. They spent almost all of a night in their small cabin, huddled together in prayer, my mother telling me later, "certain we were going to die, our bodies lost forever in the sea."

When their ship entered New York harbor, they first saw the imposing Statue of Liberty. The passengers crowded the rails to view it, many weeping and kneeling to say their prayers, a few who knew the lines from the poem by Emma Lazarus repeating them to others. At different times in the years that followed, I heard my mother and brother and sister speak of their first sight of the statue.

"I felt grateful she was a woman," my mother said. "I felt she would understand a woman's heart."

"I wondered what she was holding," my sister Barbara said. "Then I recognized it as a torch like the Olympians carried in ancient Greece."

"I had read in school about the Colossus of Rhodes," my brother Dan said. "I thought this must be the Colossus of America."

Many years later, in a letter written to me less than six months before he died, Dan mentioned a dream in which he had seen the statue. Perhaps, nearing the end of his life, his spirit returned to what he recalled as the beginning of his life in America.

But my family's entrance into America wasn't without stress and fear. Even after they had passed through the examining areas, the representative from the parish who would escort them back to Utah hadn't arrived. In the confusing exchanges with an inspector and interpreter who knew little more Greek than my father knew English, a decision to detain my family overnight was construed by my father as imprisonment. In his effort to show the officials that he wasn't a pauper and should be allowed to enter the country, my father showed them a gold coin he had carried from Greece. To authenticate its purity, he bit the metal. I saw the coin years later and it seemed to me to reveal a faint indentation from my father's bite. (Or was it the intensity of his emotion I remembered when I saw the coin?)

His protests were to no avail. They were sent to the male and female dormitories, my father with the boys, my mother with the girls. It was the first time they had ever been separated.

My father would talk later in his life about the first

night on Ellis Island as his introduction to democracy. He spent the dark, sleepless hours, frantic about my mother and the girls, hearing the snores and mutterings in strange tongues of strangers in beds around him. When the first traces of dawn lightened the sky, he rose and walked to a window. Through the bars he saw the statue that loomed in the harbor. He had seen it from the ship the day before, had been as impressed with it as the others, but he saw it that morning with a sharper definition and perception. The mist gilded the majestic head, the torch emerged like a sun from the receding night. He saw the statue suddenly as a spiritual incarnation of some ancient, beneficent goddess, sent to console him in his anguish, reassuring him that a fortuitous destiny would prevail. And, later that morning, the escort from Utah arrived and my family entered America.

This is the story I remember as I look at the photograph. In the sprawling multiplicity of nationalities and races that make up our nation now, myriad other stories are enclosed in family albums, within similar old pictures, in diaries, journals and letters. They symbolize the triumph of diversity, the persistence of a dream, the longing for a sanctuary of green leaves and of peace, of an education for one's children, and the free worship of one's faith. All of life, my father often said, was a miracle we must try to deserve each day. And the greatest miracle in his life, he told us, was to have brought his family to America.

The miracle renders insignificant the ephemeral glitter of celebrations, the minting of medallions and the plethora of gaudy and tawdry souvenirs with which we mark these events. These have nothing to do with the vision my father saw from the barred window of his compound on that misted dawn seventy years ago. He sensed the meaning of the great statue clearly then, and that is the dream each of us, sons and daughters of immigrants, grandsons and granddaughters of immigrants, must renew and fulfill in our own lives.

Memories of Easter

WHEN SPRING COMES each year and the last frosted cold and snow loosens from the crust of the ground, in that season Persephone returns from the womb of Hades, and the earth enters a cycle of fertility once more. During this rebirth, there is enacted the celebration of Easter, the most significant ritual of the Greek Orthodox Church as it is for other Christians.

The Easters of my childhood were a time of magic and anticipation, not the suspense that preceded the beribboned packages and ornamented trees of Christmas but a more mystical and haunting experience. These rituals gained added importance in my heart because my father was the priest of our parish church on South Michigan Avenue, and his vivid image dominated the whole of the Passion of Christ. I will never forget his tall, regal figure clad in the colorful and glittering vestments, leading the services of worship, his voice resounding to every corner of the church, his face glistening in the curling mist of candles and incense with the lambent glow of a prophet. And his marvelous, long, slender-fingered hands which, when he held them aloft, burst like pale flowers from the encirclement of his sleeves.

The Passion of Easter would begin with forty days of fasting. My father's fast would be stringent and relentless while ours was haphazard. But as we came closer to the beginning of Holy Week, stricter attention was paid to our abstention from eggs, cheese, milk, butter, and meat. In our classrooms we were told and retold zealously the story of Christ.

An animation and excitement communicated itself through our house, and in my mother, sisters, and brothers. My father rose earlier and returned home much later, sleeping only a few meager hours a night. In this time, despite his weariness, a vibrance radiated from him, and I understand now it was his absorption into the ritual of the Passion. He mustered his strength for the rigorous demands upon him, the hours of confession he listened to each day, the exhausting and lengthy services every night.

We moved through the early part of the week, attending church and then arriving at Holy Thursday, the night of the crucifixion, the agony of Christ on the Cross lamented and shared. All morning and afternoon of Good Friday the women and children carried baskets upon baskets of flowers to decorate the catafalque, which contained the coffin of Christ, bedecking the bier with flowers twined within flowers. Until the last hour of the Good Friday services late that night when the death of Christ was sanctified.

But all our week moved toward the great revelation of Saturday night, the night of Anastasis or Ascension. From the early part of the evening when we first entered the por-

tico of the church, whispering excitedly to our friends, pur-
chasing the long, slender white candles with the tiny paper
cups to catch the drippings of wax, we waited in a fever of
anticipation. All through the hours of the evening we
shifted restlessly in our seats. Sometimes catching the eye
of a friend, we managed to slip from our pews, past the vigilant gaze of the trustees, to gather giggling and whispering
in the washroom and corridors of the basement. Often a
trustee would zealously drive us back up to church, but
whether we were dispersed in our loitering or not, as the
final hour neared toward midnight we pushed our way back
to our places, accepting the reproving looks of the adults for
our absence. By this time the crowd filled every pew,
pressed into every corner of the church. As the last few moments before midnight elapsed, we stood thronged and
jammed together in a common bond. Perhaps the older
people remembered in those moments the Easters in their
villages in the old country, the services in small churches on
the slopes of the mountains. But for those of us too young
to have such memories, the emotion of the anticipation had
its particular flavor.

We listened to the voices of the black-robed and white-
collared girls of the choir, led by the sonorous and resonant
baritone of our choirmaster, "Mr. George." "Kyrie Eleison,
Lord Have Mercy," chanted an old man with a face like a
weathered spruce. "Kyrie Eleison," prayed the old, somber-
faced women in black. "Kyrie Eleison," chanted my father,
and the choir responded, "Kyrie Eleison, Kyrie Eleison."

At midnight, the moment we had been waiting for, the
packed and crowded church would be plunged into total

darkness. To this day I can recall the chill along my flesh as that blackness descended. For Jesus Christ was in that darkened church. I felt it in my bones, perhaps a haunted and blooded memory of the somber catacombs where our forebears gathered to whisper their prayers. Within the encompassing darkness was the presence of His thorn-crowned and tormented head stirring within the tomb.

We would draw closer together, my body pressed against my mother, drawing what comfort I could from her nearness, from the proximity of my brothers and sisters, my friends and their parents. There would be a holding of breath, a fastened silence, unbroken except for a few small children whimpering, a baby crying, an old man coughing.

Then a great exhilaration would sweep like a wind through the tense and crowded church. For before us, in the confines of the Sanctuary which contained the Altar table of marble, a single, flickering taper of flame appeared. The flame moved forward, and as it emerged from the Sanctuary, I saw my father, his hand holding aloft the candle, his face glistening and disembodied with the beauty of an angel of the Lord or a Prometheus delivering the first flame to Man.

And in the cloistered darkness of the church, it was not only our hands clasping our candles that moved toward that solitary flame but a yearning and hunger in our souls. We watched and waited impatiently as from that lone candle the first of the other candles were lit and people turned to light the candles of those around them. The flames leaped from candle to candle, from pew to pew, until the entire church was a great flowing, bobbing sea of a thousand candles, every dark recess, every hidden and shadowed corner illumined.

As my own candle was lit, I looked up at my mother and she smiled at me. I marveled at the flame in my hands, at the curlings of light and mist that trailed streamers about our heads and sent eerie shadows across the icons of the old, bearded saints. I looked up at the dome of the church where the great painted figure of God, the Father, loomed above our heads, and his stern visage seemed suddenly warm and benign.

Then we joined in the singing of the Christos Anesti, Christ is Risen, the exquisite hymn that marks the jubilant acknowledgment of the Ascension of Christ.

"Christos Anesti, ek nekron, Thanato, Thanaton patisas, kai tis en tis mnema si, zoe charisamenos."

Three times the hymn was sung, our voices rising in a great swelling chorus of jubilation.

From that moment the hymns and chants were anticlimactic, and those with small children began to leave. My mother left with one of my brothers to complete the festivities that would begin when we arrived home. I fidgeted with one of my older sisters, anticipating the banquet ahead, every moment dragging like an hour.

When the services ended and the church emptied, we emerged into the darkness of the middle hours of night. We passed little groups, families moving to their cars, shielding their still-burning candles carefully against the gusts of wind. "Christos Anesti, Christ is Risen," we called to one another. "Alithos Anesti, Truly He is Risen," we answered. When the cars pulled away, each interior was illumined by the glow of candles, a strange procession of glittering light sweeping into the gloomy neighborhoods of the city.

In our apartment the aroma from my mother's kitchen spread a savory fragrance across every room. All the weeks of fasting, however desultory or reluctant at times on our parts, blossomed suddenly into a ravenous hunger. And at the long festive table in our dining room, we sat down, relatives and friends, to the splendor of that meal. There was the thick, rich mageritsa soup made from sheep's entrails, chunks of roast lamb dripping spicy juices, hunks of warm bread, slabs of white feta cheese, dark, briny olives, and decanters of glistening amber retsina wine. At the head of our table, my father, radiating a glow that encompassed all of us despite our weariness, picked up the first of the blood-red dyed Easter eggs, throwing down the first challenge. Soon we were all cracking eggs with one another, victories and defeats sweeping us into laughter and shrill cries.

In this way we passed the remainder of the festive night, and then as the first glimmers of dawn appeared against our windows, we went to bed. And I will remember as long as I live the marvelous, satisfying, and stomach-sated weariness of those dawns when I crawled gratefully into bed, my eyelids struggling to close, benevolent daylight peeping in around the corners of the shades, and the rooms about me grown strangely, consolingly silent.

Long ago . . . so long ago. Almost thirty-five years have elapsed since then. Now as I enter the church on the Saturday night before the Ascension, most of the people I see are strangers. Those I still know are not as they were even as I am no longer as I was. We have grown into middle age together, some bald, some gray-haired, lean or portly. We greet one another, smiling a warm, lucent recognition of pleasant memories we have shared, a melancholy for the friends we have survived. That pretty girl resembles her father with whom I once played ball. That tall, handsome boy resembles his mother with whom I had once acted in the school plays. I see my sister, a widow now, my nephews with their pretty wives, my great-nephews and great-nieces around their legs.

Inside the church, in the final hour before midnight, I stand beside my mother as I did so many years ago. I tower above her now for she is grown old and white-haired, only her eyes still alert within the deep carved wrinkles of her face, her lips trembling as she follows the chanting of the hymns. On the other side of me is my wife, who as a young girl shared those memories I have of long ago, still lovely despite the first gray strands in her thick black hair. And my youngest son beside her, shifting restlessly in shirt, tie, and suit coat, his black curly hair falling about his ears. Does he yearn to slip out and descend into the basement corridors where I am sure a small group of boys chatter and laugh, wary of the trustee who may come to rout them?

As the moment of midnight approaches, the crowd swells and throngs together once more, men and women stirring in anticipation. The children push back to return to their places beside their parents. An old magic returns to possess us.

The church is plunged into darkness and in the first onslaught of blackness and silence, I am hurled suddenly into the past. A quiver of excitement spreads through my body because in a few moments the first consecrated candle will be carried from within the Sanctuary. And my father will return again, to stand before us, the flame-giver and redeemer, and from his candle a thousand candles will spring into light. My mother will grow younger and vigorous once more, age and weariness diminished from her body as she thinks of the feast to be served at home.

But even as the first candle emerges, I understand the past is gone; my father is gone, dead now some twenty years. Another good priest emerges with the candle to light our flames. Perhaps in the darkened church his own son sits, watching and listening, full of the pride and love I felt for my father.

Easter will return next year, and for as long as men live, even as Persephone emerges from the womb of the Earth. The tomb of Christ will be decked with flowers. His moments of agony and redemption will be shared again and again on the darkened midnights of the Ascension and from the solitary and consecrated first flame, the thousand candles will be lighted. The children will feel the haunting mystery of that moment even as my companions and I felt it, because it is the enigma and celebration of the rebirth of the earth itself. Even when no child I knew as a child still lives, long after I am gone, there will be those who understand that our lives are like the candles that come so fleetingly and flickeringly to life, tiny flames that we seek to shield and protect against the darkness and the wind.

Christos Anesti . . . Christ is Risen . . . O my father . . . Christos Anesti . . . O my mother . . . Christos Anesti . . . O

my wife and my sons, nephews and nieces, sisters and
brothers, companions of my youth, living and dead . . .
Christos Anesti . . . Christ is Risen . . . Truly He is Risen . . .
Truly He is Risen.

Circles of Memories
and Love

FOR A PERIOD of two years during my boyhood, the time spanning my tenth to my twelfth years, I was confined to bed for an illness that seriously affected my lungs. Although my first reaction to the doctor's edict was glee at escaping the drudgery of school, that levity was soon replaced by feelings of helplessness and fear. Ghosts lurked just beyond the rim of the lamp in my room, and Death stirred in the dark, shadowed corners.

Ordered to bed at the end of the summer, I was still able to hear the raucous, merry cries of my friends playing in the street below my windows. When they returned to school, the street grew quiet, and I longed for their voices once more. Autumn came, a melancholy and disquieting time of fading flowers and withering leaves, reflecting my own decline. With the advent of early frost, the sun grew pale and the earth chilled into desolate winter. I lay stiffly on my back in bed, wondering if my body would ever heal and whether I would regain my strength and emerge re-

stored, as the animals and foliage erupted with new life in the spring.

Our family lived, at this time, in a long, narrow city apartment with numerous bedrooms adjoining a single corridor. My days and nights were spent in a sun parlor of the apartment, a small room set with windows on three sides, in a bed where I read, ate, and slept. In addition to my father and mother, there were two brothers and three sisters, four of them older than I was, one a year younger. There was also Naka, the woman who had lived with my family since my birth, and her son.

Christmas reunited our family, my brothers and sisters returning from their sojourns at school. Illness made experiences and relationships I had always taken for granted more dear to me, and I enjoyed the noise and activity the holidays brought into the house. In some frantic, fearful way I sought to store up the warmth of the season against those days when the tedious hours would once again hang like weighty stones around my neck.

On Christmas Eve, the first December of my illness, I was carried to the old sofa in the parlor, bundled under a blanket, and allowed to watch my sisters and brothers and a few friends trim the great green and fragrant tree set on a stand in the corner. The room smelled of pine and was full of banter and gaiety, which I shared.

"Those lights are too close together. They're lopsided."

"Your head is lopsided!"

"Put the silver ornament higher."

"Hold the ladder, will you?"

"Let me up there. I'll show you how to decorate a tree."

One of my sisters prepared cups of sweet, steaming cocoa with dabs of snowy whipped cream floating on the top. As I sipped the cocoa, they transformed the bare-branched tree into a majestic pillar of lights, ornaments, and tinsel, the peak adorned by a sparkling star.

When the trimming of the tree was completed, my brothers and a couple of their friends hauled a bulky brown carton into the room.

"What's in there?" I asked.

"None of your business. Back to bed for you now."

Despite my heated protests, I was carried back to bed and warned to go to sleep. But, convinced the mysterious box had something to do with me, I lay curious and wakeful in the darkness, listening to the whispers and giggles from the other room.

Long after everyone had gone to bed, the shadowed rooms trailing the fresh, redolent scent of pine, I felt myself on the verge of some miraculous experience. Finally, weariness subduing my anticipation, I fell asleep.

On Christmas morning, my father and mother, Naka and her son, my brothers and sisters—all sleepy-eyed in pajamas and robes—crowded into my room and woke me. They stood smiling and silent while I was helped into my robe and carried again into the parlor. The lights of the tree were on, boxes of gaily wrapped presents were strewn about its trunk. And there, circling the trunk of the tree, was a silver track on which stood a gleaming electric train—a black, sleek locomotive; a chunky coal car; and a string of bright yellow passenger coaches, the cutouts of miniature figures framed by the tiny coach windows.

I was given the transformer to hold on my knees. While my family enjoyed my stunned delight, I moved the switch carefully. The stately train responded, circling the gleaming track slowly at first, gathering speed as I pushed the switch higher until, whistling like the wind, the train raced round and round the track, the coaches lurching, the wheels spinning furiously, sparks striking from the silver rails.

The train had been the main prize raffled off at the neighborhood theater where my brother and sister worked as usher and cashier. When the winner, unmarried and childless, saw the size of the box the train was in, he offered to sell it for ten dollars, less than a quarter of its cost. My brother Mike (after a hasty phone consultation with my father) made the deal and brought it home for me. So, on a raffle and another man's chance, the marvelous electric train became my treasured possession.

I played with the train through the holidays, running it round and round the shimmering tree. I made tunnels out of boxes; I created forests by lining the track with my mother's plants. At the beginning of January, when the tinsel, ornaments, and lights were taken down and packed into boxes until the following Christmas, the old tree—with a few tatters of tinsel and some flakes of artificial snow still hanging from the green boughs—was carried to the alley. The track was moved into my bedroom and connected around the foot of my bed, the transformer placed on a small board beside my pillow.

From morning until night, during the months of that winter, the train filled the hollow of my hours. I sent it on its journeys in the light of breaking day, the rays of pale, winter sun filtering weakly through the windows. I drove it in the twilight, the beam of the locomotive flashing through the shadows, lights sparkling in the tiny windows of the coaches.

In my fantasies, I was the engineer of that cannonball express, roaring across the limitless expanse of the land, speeding through valleys bordered by mountains, racing past small, sleeping towns, crossing bridges suspended over giant canyons. Riding the winged, swift fury of the train, controlling its vast power by the barest movement of my fingers, I was provided the means to flee the fear of my illness and the stifling prison of my room.

Long after I had recovered from my illness, during the Christmas holidays of later years, I would sometimes unpack the train and set up its tracks and cars. The task grew more difficult as the train became older because the tracks were bent and needed to be straightened, the locomotive light did not work, and the coal car had a broken axle. All these impediments finally made me pack the train away for good.

I forgot about it for a number of years, until one day— after I was married and had left my father's house—I was cleaning out the storeroom in the basement of a building from which my parents were about to move. There in a pile of rusted and discarded tools, I found the locomotive of my train, a shabby and battered relic. There wasn't a trace of the coal car, passenger coaches, or any sections of the track. For a moment, holding the locomotive in my hands, I remembered the wild, joyous journeys we had shared. I was tempted to keep it, but because there seemed something childish about remaining attached to a toy, I threw the useless old engine away.

One by one, as the years passed, my sisters and brothers left my father's house, beginning journeys and lives of their own. My brother Dan, who first married Penny, later married Marvel and moved to California; my sister Tasula married John Thoman and moved to live in Missouri. While in the Army overseas, my brother Mike married Carmencita. My sister Barbara married John Manta and remained in Chicago, as did my youngest sister Irene, who married Ray Fox. I married Diana, a dark-eyed sweetheart I had known since childhood. We set up housekeeping in a small kitchenette apartment on the third floor of a massive court building whose windows looked out upon a hundred identical apartments.

On the Christmas holidays, those of us in the family who still lived in Chicago gathered a few more times in my father's apartment. We repeated the childhood ritual of trimming the tree, exchanging presents, eating my mother's pilaf and chicken, and telling stories. By the end of the evening we would cluster around the ancient upright, out-of-tune piano that my sisters had studied music on when they were children. While one of my sisters played the familiar songs, we would sing in a strident chorus, my father's reedy, gentle voice leading us. I think he enjoyed the family singing together more than anything else about the day.

My father died soon after that, and I joined the members of my family who had moved away, traveling to Pittsburgh with my wife and two young sons. A third son was born to us the first year we were there.

We rented a white, clapboard house along a road that ran between a Civil War cemetery on a hill and a great forest in a valley behind us. The silence of the cemetery was disrupted in autumn by the tumult of thousands of birds gathering from all over Pennsylvania to begin their migrations.

With December, heavy snows fell across the valley of the Monongahela, blanketing the graves in the cemetery and coating the branches of the trees in the forest. We built snowmen and forts in our yard and slid down the slopes on our sleds, laboring to drag them back to the top of the hills. Each day the exhilaration of the season mounted until, on Christmas Eve, we watched our sons climb into bed, their ears straining as they listened for the rustling of reindeer and the tinkling of bells in the snow-flecked sky. And for a while then, I would share all their excitement and delight.

"Do you hear them?" one of the boys would say.

"Sure," I said.

"I don't hear anything, papa," his brother said, with disappointment in his voice. "Why don't I hear anything?"

"They're not close enough yet," I said. "But they're coming closer every minute. Listen. Can't you hear them now?"

"Yes!" he said. "Yes! I can hear them so clear now!"

There were a few years back in Chicago and then a two-year interlude in California. Our eldest son Mark had gone off to college, and my wife and our two younger sons, John and Dean, discovered that the snowless terrain of those smoggy, sunny, and hot Decembers did not seem like Christmas at all.

Far from home, we gathered a large, festive group around us on Christmas Day. In addition to my niece Barbara, her husband George, and their children Dawn and Dean, there were about a dozen Greek film actors we had come to know—character and supporting players, dwellers in furnished rooms and small apartment hotels. They brought guitars and a flute and a fevered hunger for my wife's Greek meal. Full of wine and food, they sang, laughed, and danced—each of them contributing some of the warmth they remembered from Christmas celebrations during their own childhoods. We retained them as friends during the time we remained in California. The day we left once more for the Midwest, several of them came to help us pack and load our car, and we embraced and cried as we parted.

Back home, the ritual of our family Christmas celebrations expanded because the branches of our family had grown. We were joined by our nephews and nieces, the sons and daughters of my sisters and my wife's sister. They had first come to our house as children, and they continued to celebrate with us as they grew into young adults. After they married, they came with their husbands and wives and, finally, with their own children. As our sons grew tall, the down of beards on their faces, a new influx of small boys and girls joined our holiday festivals. Over the years, the number rose from twenty to thirty to forty, a cheerful and unruly assembly, spending the day in our house in the city; then—after we moved once more—coming to our home in the Indiana Dunes, where the cold, crisp air smelled of lake and tall green pines.

For the twenty-five years we have been in this house, Christmas Day begins early, the carloads of relatives arriving in the morning. Through the day we grow expansive, shout at one another in the fashion of Greeks, play in the snow with the children, watch a football game on TV. All this time, the kitchen radiates an assortment of tantalizing fragrances. The great turkey browns in the oven, stuffed with the special dressing my wife makes the night before— ground lamb, hard bread, celery, pine nuts, onions, and oregano. As one moves through the kitchen, there becomes visible platters of glazed sweet potatoes, white and yellow cheeses, crimson cranberry jelly.

We place a long piece of plywood over our table to triple the number who can sit down to dinner. Even this enlargement does not seat us all, and smaller tables are set around the room for the children, miniature fiefdoms administered by an older child. Then I begin carving the great turkey, fighting off foragers seeking to loot a strip of succulent skin. Finally, at the table, we say the Lord's Prayer in Greek: "Pater imon, Ou en dis ouranis, Agiastito to onoma sou . . ."

From the end of the table, my mother—grandmother

and great-grandmother to most of the assembly—nods gravely in approval, urging on one of the children who might be mumbling the words.

After dinner, the children besiege us in their eagerness to get at the presents, and we begin the ceremony of passing the boxes and opening the gifts. In an hour of pandemonium, the room fills with discarded reams of tissue and wrappings—the newspaper comic pages my wife has always used to wrap our gifts. As twilight falls, we light our fire; and while wild bands of children raise a shrill chorus of voices as they play with new games in various rooms, we burn the wrappings, feeling the waves of heat glowing across our noses and cheeks.

When it is time to leave, the children grown sleepy and fretful, car after car loads up, children and their presents packed in every corner. Small faces press their noses against the glass of the windows; boys and girls wave us farewell. My wife and I stand in the driveway waving back at them until the last of the cars has gone, the final set of red taillights disappearing down the hill. For a moment we stand in silence under the frost-ridden night, the stars a panoply of splendor in the cold night sky, absorbing all the reasons we have to be grateful.

Afterwards, in the most relaxing part of the day, my wife and I sit wearily before the fire, the only other light in the room glowing from the small, colored bulbs suspended in the branches of the tree. As we have done so many times before in the years we have spent Christmas together, we recount the events of the day, sharing them between us, laughing at some specially humorous remembrance.

In those moments of firelight, the decorated tree providing its becharmed link to the past, nostalgia is difficult to resist. I remember Christmas in my father's house, my sisters and brothers, young and strong then, all of us gathered around the old, upright piano, our voices raised in chorus as my father led us in song. I remember Christmas when our sons were still small, my wife secretly wrapping their presents, filling their stockings with chocolates and hard candies. I remember the shrill, eager way they ran down the stairs in the morning. And I remember, born of the Magian night and the mesmerizing tree, the train which was my father's gift to me on a Christmas fifty years ago.

Fifty years ago . . . yet even as the relentless passage of time stirs a melancholy within my spirit, I am, in a way, reassured. For even as the beauty and magic of that train belongs to me, so in the holidays we spend together now, my sons, nephews and nieces, great-nephews and great-nieces, are provisioning their own storehouses of memories. The graceful sleep of a deaf, white cat, a sled swooping down a snow-packed hill, the old grandmother and a swarm of twenty grandchildren grinning for the camera, a music box playing some haunting refrain to be heard again in the years to come, a glimpse of a star-filled night through the boughs of a pine tree—any of these might form the core of their recollections, graced in years to come by a significance known only to them. Perhaps it will be the assembly, the memory of forty of us gathered around the long table, joined by the blood of our families, sharing the luminous warmth of the day.

I would like to believe that our lives do not run in horizontal lines, broken at the beginning and at the end, but—like the tracks of my talismanic train—in circles of memories and love. Sharing this inestimable legacy, we experience joy and a harmony with the ancient truth of Ecclesiastes, the words of the preacher, the son of David, king in Jerusalem: "One generation passeth away and another generation cometh: But the earth abideth forever."

Meanwhile, my train roars on, careening swiftly around the circle of silver track, sparks flying from the wheels, miniature figures framed in tiny squares of light, carrying me on solitary journeys across the vast, limitless night.

My train speeds on and on as long as I am the teller of the story. Tomorrow, someone else will spin the tale.

City Lights

AFTER RECOVERING from my two-year illness, I returned to the streets, surging from awkward childhood toward a graceless adolescence, in the heartland of a Chicago neighborhood that held me like a fetus nestled in a womb.

My father's church was on South Michigan and 61st Street. Studs Lonigan and his Irish roamers had come and gone from that turf that was resettled by Italians, Greeks, Blacks, and Jews. Though we sometimes evidenced a virulent prejudice against one another in those gloomy seasons of the Depression, our economic austerity transcended racial and ethnic lines.

All of us could join in envying and resenting the rare kid who owned a bicycle. The rest of us depended for locomotion on an orange box nailed to a board that moved on the split wheels of a roller skate. One foot on the board and one pumping along the sidewalk, we roared along on these dilapidated vehicles that we decorated with paint and decals, giving them names like "Comet," "Charger," "Thunderbird," all names that General Motors, Ford, and Chrysler would adopt in later years.

Our family included five of my brothers and sisters, Naka, a Swiss lady and her son who lived with us for years, and my parents. The ten of us inhabited a series of miasmic seven- and eight-room apartments in two- and three-flat buildings on Eberhart, Indiana, Vernon, and South Park. These grimly identical structures were separated from one another by narrow gangways with damp, sunless earth infested by slithery worms we dug up and dangled before horrified, shrieking girls.

The layouts of the apartments seemed diagrammed by the same brooding builder. They consisted of a front room overlooking the street, a murky parlor, a long, narrow corridor from which cramped bedrooms and small bathrooms ran off like cubicles in a cavern. The kitchens contained a battered icebox and a worn gas stove. Behind the kitchen, suspended like a crow's nest in a maze of back porches, was a little backroom with barely space enough for a dresser and a bed.

This dorsal appendage of the apartment was often my province, its ill-fitting windows useless against drafts and cold moanings of wind in winter. To be called to rise for school on one of those January or February mornings meant peering wretchedly from beneath the clump of covers into the glacial cold. Testing the temperature of the frigid air by exhaling, I fully expected to see the vapor of my breath congeal into a sphere of ice and plummet to the floor. Finally, in desperation, I would leap from my bed like a runner from the blocks and fling on my clothes.

Yet in spring and summer, with my windows open, that

room provided instant communication with my friends in the concrete courtyards and alleys below. They would shout for me to join their games and I would race downstairs.

Of all the hundreds of games we played, the one that remains most vivid for me was one thrilling contest of "Kick-the-Can." Nineteen of my playmates had been captured and imprisoned by the goalkeeper during a suspenseful and harrowing three hours. I remained the single player still free, the only one who might still liberate them all by kicking the can. From where I crouched beneath a porch I could hear their imploring voices bawling my name.

"Save us, Harry!"

"You're our last chance, Harry!"

"Help us! Help us!"

Under cover of their whoops and cries I crept stealthily from yard to yard, shinnying up a telephone pole to a garage roof. Peering down across the peak I saw the mass of my friends, the goalkeeper staring nervously in every direction but the sky. An instant later I had leaped into their startled midst to give the can a stunning, catapulting kick.

Nineteen boys and girls shrieked and roared in exultation and scattered to hide once more. The goalkeeper, a good friend of mine until that day, slumped down against a garbage can and cried. But every victim spawns a victor, and for weeks I basked in a sweet and heroic afterglow of triumph I have never been able to match in my life since.

That neighborhood was like a province within the gates of the city, its boundaries the frontier of a foreign land. We knew there was a North Side (the snotty Cub fans lived there) and that the "L" on 61st Street banged and rattled down to the Loop with its lofty Wrigley Building and Tribune Tower. But we left our neighborhood only on rare occasions, the city beyond us remaining as strange as London or Paris. Sometimes during the baseball season we took the streetcar to Comiskey Park to cheer our valorous White Sox from the bleachers. Then, on the lazy afternoons in summer, we hiked east to Jackson Park and the lake, an expanse of trees, grass and beach as splendacious as the playground of a king.

We'd sun ourselves on the beach, frolic in the water, toss balls in arcs through the air. On the misted horizon of the lake we'd catch a glimpse of a freighter bound, we were sure, for some exotic port across the world.

By the end of the day, tired and hungry, we drank Cokes and grilled hot dogs over a small wood fire. In the flicker and glow of the dying embers we discussed matters from the most mundane to the majestic journeys and adventures that lay before us. Late at night, in a motley band, we straggled noisily back to our homes.

There was a tangible warmth to our neighborhood, a contentment and pleasure that extended beyond my mother's kitchen and the closeness of our family. Walking our streets at twilight, I knew who occupied the apartments along the way. I even knew by the lights in certain windows whether my friends were at home. If I wished to speak to one of them, there wasn't any need to ring a doorbell or phone. I stood below his window and hollered up his name.

Through the summer and into the early autumn evenings, when supper was finished, families emerged to sit on the front steps or on benches and chairs. Neighbors promenading along the street paused to talk so that before every building a small, chattering group exchanged gossip, the whirl and wind of their voices floating in a beguiling chorus along the street. Sharing that sodality, one had the feeling the community linked each family as closely as the inhabitants in a village or in a tribe.

"Hello, Mrs. Asher."

"Hello, Harry. Your father and mother well?"

"Yes, they are."

"Tell your mother I got a jar of that preserve she likes. I'll send it over with Frances."

"I'll tell her."

That easy familiarity and trust extended even to the provinces of commerce—the shops along 61st Street, from grocery to delicatessen, from drugstore to clothing store. When the sneakers and jeans I wore had passed beyond mending, my mother took me to the St. Lawrence Dry-Goods store owned by old Mr. Seigel. The dimly lit store was always in total disarray, clothing in piles of mismatched sizes and shades. But Mr. Seigel knew precisely where everything was. With a swift, perceptive appraisal of how much I had grown since he fitted me the last time, he would assault some pile and tug out a pair of pants I would try on behind a screen.

"How do they fit?" my mother would ask.

"They're too big," I'd say. "I can stick my whole fist in the belt."

"He'll grow into them," Mr. Seigel would say sagely. "If they fit him just right now, they won't last the boy as long."

My mother would thank him, grateful for his concern about our finances, and we'd purchase the pants.

The years passed. My friends grew from gangling adolescents into adults. Our neighborhoods altered, residents moving away, others taking their places. My journeys to school and work moved me into the sprawl of the city. I went downstate to the University of Illinois for a while and then left school, returning to work in the South Chicago steel mills. In rapid succession afterwards I labored for a wax firm, pressed clothes for a tailor, delivered auto parts, dispatched ice trucks from a depot at 15th and Halsted.

Through these years I came to discover more of the bleakness and desolation that existed in the city. From the windows of the "L" I saw the broken, crumbling ruins of tenements. In the streets I passed the wretched and the driven, poor citizens in contrast to the elegant men and women who patronized Marshall Field's and Carson's downtown. The district around the ice depot held ragged men huddled in doorways to keep warm, swigging wine from pint bottles concealed in paper bags. The more I witnessed the city, the more I became aware of it as noisy, ugly, and unfeeling.

Even as we continued to live in apartments on the South Side, my older brothers and sisters departed, some to work, others to marry, settling in Missouri and in California. Naka died, her son left too, and only my younger sister and I remained at home with my parents. When I began courting the girl who became my wife, I traveled on the Illinois Central from South Shore to Hyde Park where she lived. We spent many evenings walking around the promontory on 55th Street, sitting on the ledges of shadowed rocks, unaware as we stared across the darkened lake that someday we would live on the opposite shore.

For a short while after we married we occupied a studio apartment in Kenwood, then returned with my parents to a house we bought together in South Shore. My father became ill soon after we moved into the house. For the first time in years I returned to the old neighborhood to visit him in the Woodlawn Hospital. We would sit together by the window of his room, sometimes talking of how we would follow the sun when he became well. Sometimes we just sat silently while he stared at the steeple of his church a few blocks away. After three months in the hospital, my father died.

In this time I was also beginning to write, making an effort to sell my stories. My wife and I and our two sons moved to Pittsburgh. My contact with Chicago became a series of items in the newspapers, and letters from family and friends. Each time I returned for a visit the city seemed changed: bigger, grander, more alien. The Wrigley Building and the Tribune Tower had been dwarfed by the Standard Oil building, the huge black tiers of the John Hancock, and, finally, the Sears Tower. Certain vestiges of the city remained unchanged. Mayor Daley still held reign, Kup wrote his daily newspaper column, and, from time to time, a bullet-riddled body was found stuffed in the trunk of a car.

One more trip away for two years, this time to Los Angeles, then we returned to the city once more. Although I had not like the seasonless pattern of days in California, I'd enjoyed the sense of space. I had also discovered an increased capacity for work in an environment that wasn't cluttered and clamorous. In search of such a place, we decided to leave the city, selecting a house on the Indiana shore of Lake Michigan. We raised our sons there, sending them to a small town school near where we shopped in stores that were reminiscent, in a way, of the neighborhoods of my childhood. We came to know the shopkeepers by their first names. As they learned our names, a familiarity of dialogue grew up, the kind of small talk no longer possible in the great malls with hundreds of stores and thousands of shoppers.

There was also a sustainment for me, as a writer, in living the slower pace of country life, watching the variable of the altering sky, the curving transience of the seasons from the golden days of summer to autumn with its rainbow raiment. I could even enjoy the solitude of a winter twilight, hearing the cajoling murmur of crickets, encouraging reflections on the passage of years. I accepted, after a while, that I would remain in the country until the end of my life.

Through the years we have lived in the dunes my trips to Chicago about fifty miles away have been frequent, for dinners with families and friends, for lectures and teaching some classes. But they are usually visits only for the day. Late at night I drive the miles back home.

Even as I appreciate the life I am living now, I remain linked to the fortunes of Chicago. Watching the Cubs, Sox, and Bears struggle, I am pleased when they win, disgruntled when they lose. I read the daily events of the city in the *Tribune* and in the *Sun-Times,* and watch the Chicago newscasters on TV, sharing the successes and enduring the humiliations when some scandal or murder is broadcast to the world.

Fifty miles away, yet I can still see the city on those nights when the winds sweep away the obscuring mists and the sinking sun leaves a plumage of color across the water. Then the skyscrapers of Chicago appear in the distance, the Sears Tower, and "Big Stan" and "Big John," the totem poles of the Marina twins, all suddenly sparkle in the gathering dusk. Even as I understand that skyscrapers are not the city, looking at them flashing and iridescent after lake and sky are dark, I feel a curious homesickness, as if I were in exile from a land where I was born and raised.

Perhaps the homesickness is simply nostalgia for those years of my childhood, born of the yearning men and women feel to return home before they die. Tempered by the years and battered by what we have been taught to believe is the real world, we learn regressions are not possible. I know my father and mother are dead, my sisters and brothers living in other states, the neutral streets and alley pavements I played on filled with other children now. My friends of that long-ago time are older, even as I am older now, some dead, many scattered across the country and the world. I understand all that.

Yet there isn't any chain of reason that can restrict imagination. In that free domain which belongs only to human beings, with that splendid and terrifying ability to structure what is absent, I make the journey back to my childhood. Guided like a voyager by the lights that gleam across the water, I return to that city alley, see my friends peering into the shadow of garages and yards for sight of my speeding and redeeming form, their shouts beseeching me toward the eternal grail of that tin can.

Afterwards, searching in the twilight for the glow of a familiar window, I ascend the stairs and enter my mother's kitchen once again, into the fragrance of warm bread and boiling soup. Inhaling that solacing aroma, from the dining room beyond the kitchen I hear the chatter and laughter of my brothers and sisters. And, finally, stalking the dawn of a Sunday morning, making my way along the streets that once led to my father's church, I glimpse his tall, straight figure striding through the shadows, his footsteps echoing from the deserted streets, fading slowly until even when I strain my ears I cannot hear them anymore.

From the darkness, the vision of the poet illuminates our path. Childhood, city, family, friends, time, work, thought, longings, journeys, home, love and death, one moves through them as memories etch deeper into the scarred and sacred regions of the heart. Until, in the end, when all is experienced and partially understood, one turns again toward the beginning.

Where across the lake, the lights of the city of my childhood glitter and flicker like some haunting and fabled phantom bidding me to remember . . . to remember and, perhaps, one day, to return. . . .

Growing Together

LAST NIGHT, when I could not sleep, something in the wind rattling the glass of our bedroom windows, something in the faint stirrings of autumn that seeped the scents of turning foliage into the room, made me remember a night at the end of another summer about fifteen years ago.

We lived in a suburb of Pittsburgh then, my wife, Diana, our sons of nine and five and a third boy born in that time, in a small house set among the lovely rolling hills of the Monongahela valley. Behind us the hills sloped down into a great woods with hundreds of thickly foliaged trees, on which, in that time of year, thousands of birds perched and sang as they gathered for their winter migrations. In front of our house the hill mounted to a crest that enclosed an old cemetery, the stone of the monuments flaked and battered by weather and time. Most of the lettering on the stones was too faded to read but, when legible, revealed names and dates from the period of the Civil War.

In the house next to ours lived a farmer turned steel-worker, a big, warm taciturn man and his hospitable and loquacious wife. They had two sons, tall, sturdy-limbed young men in their early twenties. One played football for Clemson, the other, younger, impatient with books and school, yearned to return to the land his father had abandoned when he entered the mills.

The night I remembered was one at the beginning of autumn, a month or so after Dean was born, when Diana and I attended a farewell party for our neighbor's sons. The older boy was leaving for a year's study at a college in Europe and the younger one was departing for a job on a farm in the Midwest.

We spent several festive hours laughing and drinking. Toward the end of the evening the two youths, singing and dancing a boisterous duet, their arms linked, their heads inclined against one another, re-created a performance they had apparently played many times before. Their father and mother watched them with an unmistakable sadness. In Freda's eyes was the glitter of tears. When she caught me watching her, she grimaced sheepishly and gave me a conspiratorial wink.

Diana and I went home a short while later and long after we were in bed, in the darkness of our house, I lay awake listening to the sounds of revelry and music floating faintly across the night. Around those man-made sounds I heard the chirping of birds unwilling to relinquish their excited chatter on the eve of their own journeys. After a while, a silence settled across the earth, birds and people still. A wind rose and I imagined it swirling around the tombstones and graves of the old cemetery at the crest of the hill.

In those last moments before I fell asleep, I recalled the sadness mingled with pride and love in the faces of my neighbors as they watched their sons. But with my own sons asleep and secure around me, sons too small for journeys of their own, I could not then comprehend that sadness because it was born of years and experiences I had not yet lived.

Yet, over the years that have passed since then, that memory has returned to haunt me many times. Never in the harried hours of daylight but always in the still, wakeful passage of the dark, as if there were about that night a strange, talismanic quality, containing a meaning just beyond my grasp.

We left Pittsburgh after about two years and returned to live in Chicago. We moved into an old house on the South Side of the city, near the lake, where I made my first efforts at freelance writing. Mark was about eleven then, going unwillingly to the parochial school, struggling over lessons in Greek as well as in English, unable to understand why anybody needed more than one language. "You can only use one at a time!" he said indignantly. John was just beginning the alien experiences of first grade, apprehensive and reluctant to release our hands when we left him at school. Dean was rushing from room to room, undaunted by walls and closed doors that he rammed with glee.

The house we lived in had once known days of gaslight elegance but had fallen on hard times. Like a crumbling old castle, it wore an air of somber decay, so much a haunted and forbidding enclosure that on our first Halloween, fifty small cellophane bags of candy packed for the onslaught of children making their "Trick or Treat" circuits, not one child came to ring our bell. At the end of the evening, as we were taking John up the stairs to bed, he said with tears of disappointment in his eyes, "They thought this was the witches' house."

For the next three years we lived in that old house, rising together early each day, the older boys departing for school, Diana tending Dean and trying to keep the myriad rooms in a semblance of order. I trudged to a room on the upper floor that I had converted into a study, trying to work on a second novel and some new short stories.

Without a regular income, we struggled in those years, money for utilities and food always a problem. My five-year-old car with which we had moved from Pittsburgh stood abandoned in the lot beside our house, the body aging like a discarded shell, because I could not afford insurance or plates. I delayed selling it because a story or a book sale might have replenished our fortunes at any time. Until, having delayed too long, a day came when all our family stood silent and grieving spectators as a tow truck hauled it away to a junkyard. The last sight we had was its crippled, forlorn carcass, suspended between sky and ground, dragging its rear wheels as if unwilling to leave.

A group of neighbor children had gathered to watch and as we reentered our house I heard Mark explaining to several of them, "We're getting rid of that junk because my father's getting a new Cadillac."

There were more pleasant memories of those years. In summer we played on the crowded, teeming beach, the sun baking our almost-naked bodies, the boys shrieking as they splashed in the surf. In the twilight, under a grove of trees, we barbequed hamburgers, toasted marshmallows over the dying coals, licked the sticky sweetness off our fingers, sang songs and straggled wearily home to bed.

In the winter, the beach bleak and deserted, we walked along the sand with woolen mufflers wrapped tightly around our throats and returned to the house with chilled fingers and frigid noses, thawing out over steaming cups of sweet, fragrant cocoa.

At Christmas we scouted the nearby lots provisioned with an assortment of green firs and pines, carefully appraising fullness and height. Mark and John could never agree on the same tree and as soon as one of them urged a selection upon me, the other would shout: "Look at this one over here, Pa!" When we had finally appeased all objections, we carried the tree home. Mark and John shared the point, clutching the slender peak, walking so closely together they kept stumbling over each other's feet.

For many years my wife had assembled ornaments and decorations commemorating our marriage, the birth of the boys, the sale of a story, the publication of my first book, adding these to mementos from places we had visited. Fully decorated with lights and ornaments and tinsel, the tree was more than a tree, somehow representing milestones in the life and fortunes of our family.

On Christmas Day our nieces and nephews, newly married then, would gather to open presents. Afterwards we would sit down to the succulent turkey dinner Diana had prepared, the table garnished with cranberries and crisp-crusted sweet potatoes and glistening decanters of red wine. Until, late that night, sated with an abundance of food, exhausted from the effort of pulling the children away from their toys and games and getting them to bed, Diana and I would sit for a while with only the small, multicolored lights of the tree casting a glow across our cheeks as we talked in whispers of the day.

In those moments, under the light of the tree that carried remembrances of our years, we talked of how the boys were changing, their personalities becoming more defined. A seriousness to Mark, the quiet, intent way he had of watching or listening, as if he were carefully storing information away. John's open warmth, his amiability radiating in waves upon those around him. And Dean still assembling his spirit and his limbs, a penumbral radiance about his cheeks and eyes.

After the New Year we entered the coldest, most desolate part of winter, the bleak January and February days, daylight consumed by twilight rising in early afternoon. After dinner the boys did their homework around the fireplace, pausing to argue or tell a story of their day or simply fall silent dreaming before the mesmerizing flames, watching the glowing embers collapsing with tiny sighs. Outside the wind howled off the lake but with our family drawn close to the warmth of our hearth, we felt protected and bulwarked against the invasion of the world. When the fire had succumbed to whitened ash, we went to bed, and I slipped gratefully beneath the quilts against Diana's body, consoling our shivering by joining our warmth.

When it seemed we were marooned in the arctic of a final winter, a day would come when we felt a wild leaping in our blood. Walking outdoors we smelled the fresh, faint scents of thawing earth, felt the first verdant stirrings of

47

spring, a divination of the warmth and redemption of life once more.

In those years, as the boys grew older, the constellations of birth and death were always there to remind us that to everything there was a season. The death of my sister's husband, a man we thought would live forever because of his strength. The death of Diana's father, short, stocky, ebullient shoemaker with an abundance of laughter and unlimited reserves of love for his children and grandchildren. With his passing a part of us was lost, a measure of joy and delight in holidays we used to spend together, diminished. And along with their deaths, the passing of other friends, by accidents or illness, slowly or swiftly. But to balance the deaths there were the births of children to relatives and friends, the first sight of squirming and wrinkled babies, miraculously altered when we saw them months later, grown fat and full of milk, guzzling contentedly.

If we tried to help our sons understand these cycles of life and death, we also sought to interpret for them some of the turmoil and upheavals in society, the confrontations and the demonstrations. I tried to explain the justice of the black civil rights revolution by my own feeling as a father. I had learned in the joy of their birth and watching them grow, that to worry about sons and hope even modest dreams for them was suffering enough. A father or a mother did not require the additional anguish imposed on them by prejudice.

There were events and nightmares we could not explain to our sons because we could not fathom their meanings ourselves. The savage, senseless assassinations of a president and of his brother, and of a wise and prophetic preacher who sought, like Moses, to lead his people out of bondage. Nor could we explain to our sons the meaning of a dreadful war, placing its sorrow and guilt upon our souls and, perhaps, upon the souls of generations to come. Grateful that our own children were spared, we could not be totally comforted by their survival in a world that could heedlessly destroy the sons and daughters of other parents who loved them as much as we loved our own.

Five years, ten years . . . experiences flowing together. Birthdays and holidays, tryouts for school plays and school sports, disappointments and triumphs, clothing rapidly outgrown and endless piles of wash, first girlfriends and the deepening of voices, graduations and dilemmas, a driver's permit, the first son at the wheel of a car.

Often in these years I came to realize that however different they seemed from my own youth, under their irreverent and scoffing demeanors their longings and needs were about the same as ours had been . . . altered only by their own language and set to the indescribable rhythm of their music which had to be played at a deafening pitch. And after hours of discussion that continued late into the night, I would have an eerie sense of a ritual I had shared in before, words spoken between my father and myself many years ago. I came to understand, not without sadness, that they would seek their own experiences as I had sought my own, unable to accept my counsel in the same way I had been unable to accept the exhortations of my father.

But if each generation is required to play out the same pattern with only slight variations, each preceding generation must struggle to offer them guidance. Until perhaps the only way for the youth to break free is to pull violently away.

Mark was the first son to leave our house, entering a college in southern Ohio to study drama and English. Our last sight of him on the day we drove him to school and helped him carry his belongings into his dormitory room, was his flurried, awkward goodbye. Then he hurried across the campus, his pipe clutched stiffly in his hand as if it were a scepter to ward off evil spirits. When he returned home for the holidays there were changes in him greater than we felt a few months should have realized. He was restless and impatient, anxious to get away from the house soon after he arrived. During the summers he worked or traveled across the country to visit friends. At the beginning of his junior year, arguing and pleading until we submitted, he transferred to a college in New York City. In the year that followed he experienced a love affair that ended unhappily and, soon afterwards, left school to strike out on his own.

John went through his upheavals cushioned, in a way, because he moved in a swarm of friends that streamed in and out of our house. When we sat down at the table to eat the meals Diana prepared for us all, I felt, disconcertingly, like Brigham Young gazing upon his assorted families. By the time John entered his senior year in high school, we sensed that same alienation, that impatience with our devotion, an almost frantic eagerness to flee.

However we sought to rationalize these flights, knowing that other families experienced them, as well, we could not help believing that our flaws as parents had somehow driven them away. At least these were the reasons, enigmatic and distressing, we offered one another in those hours my wife and I talked of our sons. We envisioned growing old together, a pair of aging trees on a winter plain. Meanwhile, there were books to be written, an aged mother and a young son still to be cared for, the measure of our days and nights to be lived.

But we had not lost our sons. We had been melodramatic and foolish in assuming their flight meant rejection. As time went on and they struggled to fashion their own strengths, resolve their own dilemmas, we saw and understood their need for drawing apart. But the thread of love remained, woven constantly into our lives, like the scarlet thread woven into the white sails of old-time English ships which, in case of shipwreck, enabled searchers to spot and reach quickly the scene of disaster.

Mark came back to many nights where we talked till dawn, weary yet exhilarated, the problems not resolved but an understanding and a joined strength between us. And this last summer while John studied in Yugoslavia on a foreign studies program, his letters home were nostalgic with what he remembered of our lives together. In the final sentence of one of his last letters he wrote: "I miss you all and wave to you from my mountaintop here. Like the traveling son in *How Green Was My Valley* I know that in my valley they are not gone."

Ten years . . . fifteen years . . . a passage of time bringing us where we stand now. Signs of decline all around us. My mother, surviving my father by more than twenty years, grown frail and uncertain in her gait, falling asleep over her paper. My wife, still slender and lovely, but no longer a young woman, strands of gray in her thick black hair. Less hair on my own head and new aches and pains flashing signals through my limbs. An old dog, a frisky puppy in those Pittsburgh days, grown rheumatic, limping from room to room, finally put to sleep at the beginning of her sixteenth year.

And our sons grown to young men, twenty-four, twenty, and fourteen, the older boys bearded and mustached, shaggy apparitions appearing from time to time at our door, returning from sojourns in another city, from semesters at school, from summers overseas, hiking and wandering. Only Dean still lives with us at home.

At those rare moments now when we are all together, sitting around the table once again as we did when they were children, they laugh, still argue, display spirits and minds of their own, sharing the stories and experiences and meanings they have discovered for themselves.

I am grateful for the signs of their maturing and of renewed purpose, sharing their small triumphs and joys with as much delight as if they were my own. At the same time I catch glimpses in their faces of private griefs we can no longer share, problems they must resolve themselves.

But the eyes of our youngest son, black hair curling about his ears, see no problems or dilemma, as he listens to his brothers, his face revealing only his eager restlessness to begin journeys of his own. In those moments I look across the table at Diana. With a faint tremulous smile she answers me, affirming she has seen and understood, perhaps with more poignance than I am able to feel because they were cleaved from her flesh.

Now, in the heart of the night, the same stars glittering above me, but fifteen years added to my life, I understand what I could not fathom that night in Pittsburgh when our neighbors gave the farewell party for their sons: how almost all of life is made up of journeys, beginning with our own departures from our parents' houses, our leavetakings and homecomings, the decampments of our sons and daughters, the migration of birds over the track of forest and mountains, the swoopings of wind crossing and recrossing the land, all the recurring voyages and flights and partings carrying us toward that vast silence wherein we make the final, irrevocable journey each of us must travel alone.

For movement and change are the wellsprings of life, each age forced to recognize and accept anew the irredeemable truth that one generation passes, another generation rises, and the earth, the strange, enigmatic earth burned with the suns of fire and love, the earth endures. . . .

A Writer to His Sons

IT IS LATE at night and our house is quiet. I have walked through your rooms to cover you because the wind is cold and the old house is drafty. Your mother is asleep and I am ready to go to bed myself but the wind and the night have stirred in me a vague and disquieting unrest. So, for a little while I will wander like one of Seneca's prologizing ghosts suspended between heaven and earth.

I remember with pleasure the jubilant way we wrestled before supper and how even little Dean and the dog took sides. The way we talked as we walked along the beach and skimmed stones into the surf. The work I have done today on my novel and wondering how many more times it will have to be done before it comes right. In the quiet of the sleeping house I am sorry I hollered at John for bouncing the ball in the kitchen and regret I did not spend more time with Mark on his problems for school.

I am thirty-seven years old. This is certainly still a time of vigor and yet years enough have passed so that I can no longer excuse anything I do because of youth or innocence. Although I have worked at many different things in the past I am most of all a writer—one who has been writing earnestly for fourteen years, has published for five, and for the past two has been trying to sustain our family while writing full time.

You well know we have been living low on the bone while I work to finish the new novel. We exist on the proceeds of a story sale now and then and on a few writing assignments and a little money from lecturing. And while we can honestly be grateful that we have never gone hungry or been without a roof over our heads, there are other elements which cast a shadow.

We have no savings. The car grown old and weary with the insurance lapsed and bearing last year's plates stands dusty and motionless in the yard with the rocker panels rusting away. There is orthodontic work for Mark that we have delayed beginning and that we must start. In order to do this we must make still another loan on our burdened insurance.

I know that some of our anxieties rub off on you. There are many things your classmates have that you have to be denied. I believe many of these deprivations are compensated for by the closeness of our family life, but you must sometimes think it heartless that I lock myself into my room to write when many of our economic problems would be solved if I found a steady job like the fathers of countless boys you know.

I have chosen this night of wind and unrest to begin to write this to you because I am naive enough to think that if I write from my heart and from my love, someday, for an instant through the scatter of words you may see the sheer mountain face of my life. That is all you might have in place of any legacy of material possessions I might leave you.

You will remember that we have stood beside your grandfather's grave and I have spoken to you of life and death as an inescapable perimeter around our dreams. I told you that as I spoke to you beside his grave, you would someday speak to your sons beside my grave. And if there were in my words a bitter sense of life as fleeting and transitory then I hope time may relieve your distress.

When I was very young I could not imagine that a day would ever come when I might not spring with jubilant anticipation from my bed in the morning. I could not believe that I would endure, even on rare occasions, a sense of futility in having to struggle through another day.

But I have felt and begun to understand these things and I can therefore envision a period, perhaps twenty-five or thirty years away, when I might not think of death fearfully or unkindly. Certainly not yearn for it, but regard it as a beneficent reward, a rest after a zestful journey through life.

So much for death. Understand that it is there, and then live life as completely as you can. For me there are books to be written, stories to be told, things to be done, and places to be seen. I want above all to see you boys grow, body and soul together, into eager and bright young men, good in athletics and better in studies. I want to meet your friends and play my role as benign father. I want to see you married to girls of your own choosing, and raising families of your own. I want to see what my grandchildren will be like.

Now these are things that every father wants. If I am similar in this, why should the general direction of my days run along a different road? I would have no answer except to say that I am a writer, have always wanted to be a writer, and will write until I die.

Many fathers in countries all over the world ask no more than to be able to provide a bare security for their families. Within the more abundant provisions of our society I would like enough economic security to take care of your needs through your years of growing up and, at the same time, continue to write. Yet I know the years to come might find me no closer to that goal than I am now. I should develop into a better writer, but as far as wealth and fame are concerned, I might still be no more than another able teller of stories, published here and there in many good magazines, but in general still too bawdy for the *Ladies' Home Journal*, too exuberant for *The New Yorker*, and too square for the *Evergreen Review*.

If this is so and you wonder why I continue to write, I do so because I wish to live as a balanced human being, reasonably free from frustration and doubt, and have begun to understand that, for me, this cannot be accomplished in any other way. We cannot all live our lives like mighty pageant figures fit for noble tragedies. We cannot all chase Ahab's whale or listen to Job's voice in the whirlwind or stand like Odysseus on the burning corpse of Troy.

In my own span of years I know I have made numerous

mistakes, blundered and floundered, spoken when I should have been silent and been silent when I should have spoken. For many years I have struggled abortively to allot the proper portions of love and compassion and good sense in the reliable way an apothecary measures ingredients for a prescription. As hotly as I would like to deny it, I have eaten many meals at that great table set for fools. And the only consolation is that whatever I have learned, I feel, has not been lost.

There are those who say the writer continues in an infantile fixation to ponder the problems of life instead of living them, and others, equally as ponderous, who evaluate the creative process as narcissism, inhibition, and a failure to adjust to reality. There may be some shredded truth in this and, also, the writer may be driven by intricate variations on a theme of vanity and the glitter of fame. But these appraisals fall short. Writing is hard work and fanciful dreams of glory and neurotic release soon seek other outlets.

I think the honest writer produces because he is impelled to express the paradox of the tragedy of life with its calling trumpets and its silences. If the uncertainty of the future in an atomic age renders him full of foreboding, his answer, willful and relentless, is to achieve something that will endure.

I know I have a responsibility to provide for my family and realize that my years of irregular employment at various jobs have deprived us of any foundation of economic security. But it seems to me there is no other feasible way.

I am still not convinced of the sensibility of full-time

commitment to some job and writing on whatever time and energy is left, despite the fact that there are many writers who do both and produce competent work. I have done this at various times for years and find it a burden I would not object to sustaining except that it affects the quality of my writing. And because many of us are not supermen, working also becomes a temptation to seek security and promotion.

There is not only the lure and consolation of a steady check but the cornucopia of benefits: health and welfare plans, group hospitalization, life insurance, sickness insurance, old age and retirement insurance, profit sharing plans, bonuses, and all the rest. I am not against the apparent security they offer. However, I have lived long enough to know something of myself and my motivations and understand that when a man abandons his reason for existence in a world where integrity is a tenuous thing, he cannot provide those he loves with any emotional security although he deluges them under a wealth of bonus and insurance.

If I place such value upon writing and upon being allowed to write without rendering divided allegiance to another kind of work, you may well ask what kind of writer your father is. A fair question and one posterity generally reserves the right to answer. For the present, although a claim to genius might render my position much more formidable, I suspect that is not my cup of tea. I have many moments when I feel I have assembled passages of stirring eloquence and instances where I believe I have rendered some aspect of character and scene in stunning clarity. Against these are the other moments when I am clumsy and mute and nothing seems to come right.

I suppose what I am saying is that I don't honestly know where I stand in the literary tradition and don't much care. I have sought to tell my stories clearly, to render the tragedy, fragility, beauty, and laughter of life.

I have no kind word, whether they are good providers or not, for the writers who falsify and prefabricate, who offer the superficial cliché and who cater to the vogue of the moment, who ornament popular illusions to reap bounty of their own.

In all of this verbiage I suppose I am saying no more than that I must live right with myself and hope that in the long run this may be the best for you. I will try to appease you by a reminder that we may someday, somehow, find ourselves launched together into the Valhalla of a sale to a book club or to the movies, although I suspect there will be many problems then as well.

Meanwhile, we can walk along the beach and skim stones into the surf, and wrestle before supper, and make popcorn to eat while we watch *Twilight Zone* on Friday night. We will talk together lying across your beds at night and, if I don't have all the answers, I will try to point you in the right direction, using whatever understanding has accrued to me thus far. I want you not to be afraid to regard life with compassion. There are those who say it is an unmanly trait, but I think the world could use much more of it. Compassion, not as pity alone, but as an honest feeling for another's sorrow and hardship that leads to help. Compassion as a realization that the spirit of men and women should be revered and their bodies respected.

On the whole, and after rereading what I have written,

perhaps my reflection might hold less pertinence for you than I anticipated. I do not have any right to expect that you will cherish my words but only that you will someday understand them and therefore understand a little of me. I do not write to excuse my numerous follies. If, in places, I have given an impression of unflagging confidence and resourceful dedication, it is not wholly the truth. There are many times when my courage fails, when I grievously echo with Ecclesiastes that all is vanity and vexation of the spirit.

When I was young I wanted all the radiant earth and could not be convinced that someday I would not have it. Now it would almost be enough to have your love and respect, the affection of my friends, and the understanding of men and women who read what I write. I realize, too, that if nothing beyond these things can be achieved before I die, I will have done surprisingly well indeed.

The Life and Death of
Two Mothers

BOTH WOMEN were small in stature, less than five feet tall. For most of her life my mother was very stout. My wife's mother—we called her "Yiayia," which is Greek for grandmother—was lean. Both women could use words as awesome weapons, my mother with carefully chosen phrases that stung like a rapier, Yiayia with a few virulent invectives that landed like the blows of a sledgehammer.

Both women had a number of miscarriages and ten living children between them. My mother had six and Yiayia four, one of whom, her first son, died at the age of four. Both women outlived their husbands by many years. My mother survived my father by twenty-eight years, dying at the age of ninety in 1979. Yiayia survived her husband by twenty years and died at ninety-one in 1989.

Both women came to America as immigrants and faced the obstacles of language and alien customs. Because my mother was educated, she was able to overcome society's barriers. Yiayia was not as fortunate. She never learned to read or write and represented that legion of women who, because of gender and prejudice, never achieve their potential. Yet despite hardships and suffering, both women endured because of their unquestioning faith in God and implicit trust about their place in His cosmos.

My mother emigrated from the island of Crete in 1916 with my father, a Greek orthodox priest, and four children, two of my brothers and two of my sisters. (A younger sister and I were born some years later.) A community of young immigrant Cretan coal miners in Price, Utah, had built a church and for a year had petitioned the bishop in Crete to send them a priest with a family. The bishop selected my father, and after my parents spent months struggling with the decision, they consented to make the journey.

America was on the verge of entering the First World War in Europe, and several times on the voyage from Crete to America my family witnessed the menacing German U-boats circling their ship. After they landed at Ellis Island, a representative from the church in Utah accompanied them by train to Salt Lake City, from where they would travel by car to Price.

In the railroad station in Salt Lake City, my family was met by a multitude of almost one thousand miners who had come from towns as far as one hundred miles away to greet them with a celebratory thunder of gunshots fired into the air.

In later years my mother spoke of being terrified by the gunfire, worrying about the barbaric society her family was entering. Then she descended from the train with my sisters in their lace-fringed white dresses, and a reverential hush fell over the assembled men, who had not seen a Cretan woman or Cretan children since leaving their island. Men knelt and prayed in gratefulness, and some wept and reached gently to touch the hem of my mother's dress as she passed.

Yiayia had been born in a small mountain village called Mavriki in the Peloponnesus of Greece. The village, whose poor inhabitants wrenched a meager living from their fields and livestock, had a one-room schoolhouse that, in those unenlightened days, could be attended only by village boys. It was felt that girls who would become wives and mothers had no need of schooling. Yiayia, obdurate even as a child, refused to accept that restriction. She spent hours crouched outside the open window of the schoolhouse memorizing the songs and poems she heard the boys reciting in the classroom. Eighty years later, in the hospital where she died, she could still recite the poems she had learned while eavesdropping as a girl.

All her life Yiayia burned with resentment because she had been denied an education. She understood that she had a natural brightness that would have flourished with learning. But not being able to read or write left her with a simmering anger that in later years would result in embittered, senseless tirades, which she launched at the slightest provocation.

Two of Yiayia's brothers already had emigrated from the village to Chicago. One was married and another was a bachelor. At the urging of their parents, who hoped her brothers might find her a husband in the new world, the young men brought their seventeen-year-old sister to America. She lived with the married brother for several years, little by little doing more of the household work. Finally, on a day when Yiayia was washing clothes in a basement tub, she was seen by a young Greek from a village near her own, who was visiting her brothers.

John Perparos was an exuberant young dandy, and Yiayia was attracted to him, as he was to her. Her brothers weren't enthusiastic about him as a suitor because he was penniless, but they were also afraid a better one might not be found and they consented to their sister's wishes. The marriage, which produced two sons and two daughters, proved durable, although her husband's gentle and light-hearted nature was in stark contrast to Yiayia's temperament. Her unhappy upbringing and the death of their first son darkened her already somber nature and for the remainder of her life confirmed her stark and forbidding assessment of the human condition.

From Utah, my family moved to another parish in Savannah, Georgia, and then to St. Louis and, finally, in 1923, to Chicago. My mother, Presbytera Stella, was better educated than most other Greek women. She organized and then led societies. In the First World War she zealously sold Liberty Bonds. She also began an association with the Red Cross that she maintained as a volunteer for sixty-five years.

During the Second World War she organized efforts on behalf of Greek War Relief and Russian War Relief and formed a society whose members met to send letters and packages to young Greek-American servicemen overseas.

Yet she still managed time to look after the poor and the hungry in the parish, bringing them baskets of food or soliciting other assistance for them. She also provided them with a wise and understanding heart. Although she was a devoted parent, she never allowed parenthood to interfere with her dedication to service.

Yiayia joined a few organizations, such as the Red Cross and the parish mother's society, at the urging of my mother. Yiayia was a skilled seamstress and a fine cook. She baked faithfully for assorted events, but she never really took an active role in the administration of the societies. Perhaps that avoidance resulted from her self-consciousness about her inability to read and write.

Having always lived in apartments, Yiayia and my father-in-law in the 1950s finally bought a modest bungalow on the South Side of Chicago. They never moved again and, after his death, the house and its yard became the boundaries of Yiayia's existence. In the last decade of her life, the only time she left the house was when someone in the family took her to the doctor for a hay-fever shot or to the dentist.

Unlike most city gardeners, Yiayia was more of a farmer. She waited impatiently all winter for the planting season, growing pale and moving painfully because of her severe arthritis. With the first spring sun she'd descend gratefully into her yard, uncovering rickety old tools held together by tape, and uncoiling worn garden hoses. As soon as the ground loosened sufficiently from the frigid grip of winter, she'd attack it with a pitchfork in preparation before planting vegetables and an assortment of bulbs and seeds. The first flowerings appeared and the bare earth of the yard would disappear within a tangle of stunning flowers, stalks of corn, vines of tomatoes, beans, lettuce, onions. Everything that gnarled, lean and tiny woman touched burst into resplendent fruition.

Meanwhile, her face and arms would darken to a deep brown from the hours she spent in the sun. As if she enjoyed a mystical bond with the sun and earth, the absorption of those ancient, therapeutic rays seemed to infuse her with a strength and vigor. By her labors she linked those two primal elements into a chain of life that allowed her to metabolize their power and fertility within her own body.

All their lives both women occupied a precarious niche a step above poverty. My mother, the wife of a poor parish priest, was forever scraping and scrimping to provide her children with whatever they needed for school and work. She never went to a beauty shop in her life; she washed her long hair at home, and brushed it and then tied it up into a bun. Her dresses and hats were purchased for their utilitarian value. She wore them until they wore out, heedless of any innovation in the world of fashion.

During the Second World War, in an effort to supplement our sparse family finances as well as to make her own contribution to the war effort, my mother went to work in a downtown factory that had been converted to an assembly line making bullets. She worked the night shift from midnight to 7 a.m., and I remember waking in the early morning about the time she returned wearily home. She did not lie down to sleep but washed and changed her clothing and started the activities of her day. This overly ambitious regimen came to an end when, after being warned several times by the shop foreman, she was discharged for recurringly falling asleep at her bench. My mother indignantly denied that accusation, but I suspect the grievance of her foreman was true. She had to sleep somewhere.

Yiayia had known some affluence for a few years when her family of two girls and a boy were small children. Her husband had acquired a half dozen shoe repair and cleaning shops in the South Side neighborhood of Hyde Park. But the Depression and a pair of disastrous fires, for which he lacked adequate insurance, leveled the family to a condition of near-poverty. So my mother never had any money, and Yiayia had it briefly and then lost it. In the end both women were frugal and careful about any funds that came into their hands.

My mother spent most of the years after my father's death living with my wife Diana and me. There were five other children in her family, but I was the only son living in Chicago, and she took for granted she would live with me. She was a strong-willed woman, never rude or coarse in her words or manner, but resolved that my wife and I, as well as our sons, should follow a righteous path of faith and service. She nagged us about attending church and sought to involve us in community social affairs.

Yiayia scorned strangers and rarely answered her front bell. When a family member decided to drop by, we'd have to phone her first or she wouldn't open the door. I can remember a score of times hammering and banging on windows of her house to gain her attention.

Yiayia's acerbic nature also caused her to quarrel with her neighbors. When the lady in a much more elegant house next door to Yiayia's put up a stout wooden fence, Yiayia complained because the rough wood surface faced her yard. She was also convinced that the fence violated her lot line, and when the workmen were building it, she sat down, holding a pitchfork, on a chair directly in their path, refusing adamantly to move until the police had to be called. As tiny as she was, even the police officers who answered the call were wary of the pitchfork and her flashing, outraged eyes. The fence was completed, but for Yiayia it remained forever a source of grievance.

In the late 1960s when my wife, sons, and I moved to California for a period of two years, we left my mother in our house with a young Greek couple. During our absence she grew lonely and depressed. She came to California to visit us for a week and remained a month. Only after we had returned to Chicago and resumed our place with her, did her melancholy improve. By that time my wife and I had decided we would buy a house in the dunes of Northwest Indiana.

My mother did not wish to abandon the city, nor could she continue living in our city house alone. Eventually, in spite of her reluctance to be isolated from her activities and her church, my mother moved with us to Indiana. She was never happy there, seeing our cherished view of the lake as a panorama of desolation without the saving grace of people.

By the early 1970s, my mother's physical condition grew slowly worse. From time to time I'd drive her into Chicago to church or to a session of her Red Cross bandage unit that met in one of the church anterooms. The women would greet her warmly and for the few hours she shared with her cronies, her mood would brighten and she'd zestfully join the conversation and the laughter. About that time, one of our sons became ill in college with hepatitis and came home to recuperate. The months of inactivity waiting to get better, worrying about his health, precipitated a depression. For almost a year we had both our son ailing and my mother in declining health.

To relieve the pressure in our house, my nephews and their wives agreed to have my mother stay a month with each of them. We moved her first to the home of our youngest nephew, Steve. His wife, Dena, was a compassionate woman who endeavored to make my mother feel at home. But my mother was homesick for us, and uncomfortable in the strange surroundings. In her first two weeks she fell twice. She went into the hospital, and when she was ready to be discharged, after a few recuperative days with my widowed sister who lived in a small apartment, we made arrangements for my wife and younger sister Irene to fly my mother to the home of another sister, Tasula, in Independence, Missouri. That was just before Christmas, and each night my mother would phone us and repeat the same questions: How were we? How were the boys, our sons? Was there any community news to pass on to her? Accustomed to the large Christmas celebrations that brought thirty to forty of our relatives to our Indiana house, she spent that Christmas quietly with my sister and her husband.

Shortly before New Year, my mother became ill again in Independence and was admitted to the hospital. She developed a virulent pneumonia and almost died, which would have spared her the unhappy years that followed.

After she was discharged, grown frail and weakened, she needed more care than any of us could provide.

We brought her back to Chicago and placed her in a nursing facility we found for her in the city. On the day we moved her into the home, my brother Dan, the first of her children born in Crete, died in California. There had always been a special bond between him and my mother.

In the little more than four years that my mother spent in the nursing facility before she died, we never revealed to her the news of my brother's death. From time to time I'd bring her an imaginary letter from my brother and read it to her, telling her how well he was doing and all the happy events transpiring in his life.

My mother succumbed slowly to the paralyzing routine and hopelessness of the nursing home, growing more disoriented while still retaining some light at the summit. She'd have moments of great lucidity, when she'd ask about various members of the family, as well as how my own life was going. At other times her mind wandered back to her childhood, to her parents and sisters in the village in Crete where she had been born. My wife, my sister, or I would sit beside her while memories of the past tangled about us. At night, after we had washed her and helped her into bed and drew up the guardrail, the ritual of our departure remained the same. She would look up and say quietly, pensively, "God bless you, my children."

My mother died in May of 1979. One morning she tried to climb out of bed around the guardrail and slipped and fell, precipitating a stroke. For the following two days my wife, sister and other family members and I stood vigil. In the beginning my mother knew we were there, and, while unable to speak, pressed our hands, and with her eyes sought to communicate some indefinable emotion. Slowly she slipped more deeply into the coma that often precedes death, when consciousness recedes while the body struggles. She died on the evening before her ninetieth birthday, shortly after my wife and I had left her to go home.

As my mother blazed a trail for so many women in her life, so in death she was again a pioneer. The church trustees granted her the rare honor for any woman of being allowed to lie in state in our church, something usually permitted only to priests, bishops and the most distinguished laymen. For two days hundreds of people walked by her coffin to pay their final respects. My sons, another brother and my nephews joined me beside her coffin to greet the mourners who passed. I heard a score of new stories regarding her kindness to others. One woman told me how my mother had gone to court with her when her son was on trial. Another woman related my mother's successful intervention when her parents wished to marry her off to a much older man. A man told of her visiting him daily while he was in the hospital.

We buried my mother in the South Side cemetery beside my father, and beside the grave of my older brother, the son that to the end of her life she believed was still alive.

In the years after my mother's death, Yiayia's physical condition also worsened, but she went to great pains to conceal it from us. She would not tell us she had fallen, although we could see the bruises. When she was sufficiently frightened by her growing instability, she allowed us to take her to a doctor who, after x-rays, diagnosed blood clots that had to be operated on at once because any kind of fall might cause them to kill her.

Against her will, we managed to get Yiayia admitted to the hospital. Even after the nurses coaxed her into donning a hospital gown, she sat stiffly erect in her bed, clutching her purse and her cane, a small, solitary figure pitted against the world. When a nurse or doctor ventured too close, she threatened them with her cane. She demanded that we get her discharged, brushing aside all our efforts at explaining why she had to have the surgery. She simply wouldn't listen. On the pretext of embracing him, she called one of my sons to her side. Holding him tightly, she slipped a ten-dollar bill into his hand and whispered to him to call her a taxi.

Those hours in the hospital, anguished and alone, she took refuge in the poetry and songs she had learned as a child, reciting and singing them softly under her breath to alleviate her terror. Once, about to enter her hospital room, I saw her through the partly opened door rocking slowly back and forth in her bed in the posture of a mourner, praying to her God. In that moment of revelation I saw her as a figure resembling Job, an anachronism belonging to a time when nothing that was man-made intruded between a mortal and God. Yiayia's Earth, like the Earth on which Job lived, was devoid of books, art, music, the advances in medicine, the pageantry of history. As there was only Job and his God, so there existed in that moment only Yiayia and her God. Her questions had to be the same simple, anguished

73

ones that Job asked. Why was she being punished? Why was her God forsaking her?

After her surgery, Yiayia came to our home in Indiana for several months of convalescence. She wasn't any happier there than my mother had been. Whatever efforts we made to draw her into the circle of the family, she maintained a brooding silence. She sat with us at dinner, ate slowly and carefully, did not speak, resisting our efforts to draw her into any conversation. When I asked once why she was so depressed, with her eyes flashing, she spit her response: "If you were my age, your body rotting away into a pitiful wreck, your legs unable to hold you up to walk, wouldn't you be depressed too?"

When she wasn't in bed, she pushed her walker doggedly from room to room, pausing sometimes to sit by one of the windows. For hours at a time she remained motionless, staring intently at a bird or a flower.

Once with her daughters, son, and several grandchildren present, we offered Yiayia an eloquent exposition of why we wanted her to remain with us. She looked at us with her lip slightly curled and crisply banished all our rhetoric by uttering a simple, emphatic "Goodbye!"

We finally gave in and took Yiayia home. As we helped her up the front steps and she reached the porch, she leaned forward and fervently kissed the frame of the door. "My house . . . ," she whispered.

But her decline was irrevocable and she could no longer muster the strength or balance to walk. It was impossible for her to live alone. We brought her back to our house. She could no longer even go to the bathroom without assistance and that condition of helplessness filled her with misery and frustration.

In the middle of December Yiayia developed a cold that settled harshly in her chest. She began to run a fever and an ambulance had to be called to take her to the hospital in Valparaiso. Finally, in a week in December when heavy snow and frigid cold beset the Earth, I visited Yiayia for the last time. I sat at the foot of her bed, and watched a nurse comb her hair. I made an effort then to explain what she already understood, that we could not properly look after her at home, that my wife would become ill herself. I brought up the matter of a nursing home, something, after witnessing my mother's last years, that none of us really wanted but felt was the only alternative. Yiayia listened calmly, appearing to understand the logic of what I was saying, seeming tranquilly to accept it.

But I believe now the reason she was calm was that she had made up her mind to die. She had begun refusing food and, slowly, was slipping into an emotional solitude that banished any remaining hope or fear. When I left the hospital that night, my last sight of her frail, withered figure was of a tiny woman almost lost in the big bed, her hair neatly brushed and tied with a ribbon, her fine features creased into a slight reassuring smile as she waved goodbye.

The following day we heard from the hospital that Yiayia had died, on a day when more snow fell across northwest Indiana and the temperature hovered near zero.

It may be true that the decline and death of my mother and Yiayia were without dignity. But the irreversible wreckage of old age rarely permits dignity. In his book *How We Die*, Dr. Sherwin Nuland wrote, "The greatest dignity to be found in death is the dignity of the life that preceded it." That observation consoled me because their lives glowed with dignity.

My mother and Yiayia never had to ask the eternal questions posed by Lear and Oedipus: "Who am I?" "What is Man?" "What is my purpose on Earth?" Secure in their faith, they sought to train us as children in the ways we should walk so that when we were old we would not depart from that righteous path. They comforted our afflictions and consoled our despair. Only after they were gone were we brought face-to-face with the measure of our days and an understanding of how frail we truly were.

The image I will retain of my mother for as long as I live is of someone with a deeply felt compassion for the wounds of common experience, for all the injuries and insults that human flesh is heir to. My vision of Yiayia is of a solitary, lightning-scorched tree that existed alone, sustained by its own roots and strength.

If it is also true that death is the portion of life which a man or woman leaves unused, in the end both my mother and Yiayia left only the worn shells of their perishing, waning bodies, which their unconquerable, unquenchable spirits had inhabited so well for so long.

◾ COMMUNITY ◿

A Leap of Faith

THE POET-NATURALIST Barry Lopez, in one of his fine, lyrical books, writes that among several Indian tribes on the northern plains, the passage of time from one year to another was marked by a single, memorable event. The sequence of such memories, recorded pictographically on a buffalo robe or spoken aloud, was called a winter count.

That style of remembering and recording seems meaningful to me although my childhood wasn't spent among Indians. The fleet companions of my youth were not Sioux or Pawnee but the sons and daughters of immigrants who had come to America from Greece, Poland, Russia, and Italy. The terrain over which we roamed wasn't the plains but the building-cluttered landscape of the neighborhoods encircling my father's parish church on the south side of Chicago. We lived not in teepees but in bleakly identical two- and three-flat buildings that lined street after street. Each of these long, narrow abodes had a myriad of small rooms and a long corridor, designed, it seemed to me then, by unhappy architects whose intention was to eliminate as much warmth and light from the apartments as possible. An enigma for me in my childhood was why every bedroom window had to look out on the brick wall of the building next door.

But our neighborhood was a city within the city, with a tangible warmth that came of knowing who lived in the buildings around us. I still recall with poignancy the back porches of the apartments on balmy summer evenings, the arabesque of stairs and railings hidden in darkness softened by the murmur of voices and laughter. On different levels people would sit and talk, and the clinking of bottles and glasses would float across the night. From time to time a kitchen door opened with a fleeting glimpse of light before darkness returned. Late at night, after most of the porch-sitters had gone to bed, I lingered in the silence so I could watch the stars.

Although our ethnic backgrounds were varied, the Depression battered us into a loose-knit democracy. We did not distinguish one another by ethnic divisions but by the more tribal assessments of the handsome and the homely, the swift and the slow, the heroic and the cowardly, the kindly and the cruel.

Cruelty chiseled my winter count for one particular year, in the person of a neighborhood bully named Petros. Although only about a year older than a number of us who played together, he was bigger and stronger than any of us. His persecutions were without any ethnic prejudice. All of us suffered randomly until, for a reason unknown to me to this day, he found me the way a wolf finds a rabbit.

For weeks each time I left our apartment, I apprehensively scanned the street. The shadow of his menace hung across my games. One moment I'd be running and laughing with my companions, and then Petros would appear, accompanied by one or more girls he was always zealous to impress. He'd begin by verbally abusing me, taunting and berating me, hoping to incite me to anger so I'd attack him and he could properly beat me up. But he had bloodied my nose and bruised me enough times for me to confirm his superior strength. So I endured my agony and concealed my fury. Frustrated and impatient, he'd finally slap me down to the ground, pushing me back several times as I tried vainly to rise. Others who had experienced his cruelty turned away, sympathetic toward me but grateful they were not the victim.

I'm not sure at what point I decided that if I couldn't be spared the tormenting of Petros, life wasn't worth living. In my desperation a wild conception was born. The next time Petros began abusing me before my companions, I cried out a challenge. I dared him to match his courage against mine by having both of us jump from the third-floor porch of the apartment building in which my family lived.

My friends were awed and Petros was confused, secretly hoping my dare was bravado. When my grim face denoted I meant what I said, he had no recourse before the others but to accept my challenge. We set a time for our jump later that afternoon.

By the appointed hour a hundred girls and boys from our own neighborhood and from adjoining neighborhoods gathered in my backyard. Many of them ascended the stairs and peered down over the third-floor railing. The tension mounted as small groups of spectators whispered and pointed at Petros and me. A boy whose mother worked as a cleaning woman in the nearby hospital was designated to call an ambulance if that became necessary. A few of my friends sought to warn me that I could be crippled or killed. But even as I trembled at what I was about to do, I remained resolute.

Petros displayed a pallor and nervousness that mollified my own terror. When the appointed hour came, I recklessly told him I would jump first. If anything happened to me, I made him vow before a hundred witnesses, he had to jump anyway.

I started up the stairs, feeling like a condemned man walking his last mile. My apartment was on the second floor, and for an unbalanced moment I considered fleeing to hide inside. But I knew I'd never be able to venture to the street again so I kept climbing. From the third-floor porch I felt myself at the pinnacle of the world (like the skyscraper from which King Kong made his last swing).

Far below me the boys and girls had formed a wide circle so I had plenty of space in which to land. They stared up at me in silence and awe. I murmured a small, swift prayer and then, fearful that any delay would cause my terror to immobilize me, I clambered over the railing and jumped.

To this day I don't know what divine or mythic force protected my mad leap. Perhaps the old Greek heroes who admired boldness petitioned gravity in my defense. I plunged through the air and landed with tremendous impact on the hard dirt of the yard. I felt my legs crumble beneath me and I sprawled on the ground. For a stunned instant I lay inert, wondering if I was dying or how many of my bones might be broken. Then a dozen pairs of hands helped me to my feet. I rose and stood alone. A great jubilant roar swept the yard. Afterwards, everyone grew quiet and, with joy and anticipation on almost every countenance, they stared at Petros.

If ever a human face reflected total despair, it was the visage of the bully at that moment, shorn of any hope, depleted of any courage. I had jumped and survived and it was his turn. If he refused to jump he'd be branded forever as a weakling and a coward. But so pent up was the rage his cruelty to so many others had generated that if he hadn't jumped, a score of boys would have leaped on him and beaten him to a pulp.

Slowly, agonizingly, he began to climb the stairs. Every step he ascended provided me a quiver of delight, every landing granted me a redemption for the times he had abused me. He reached the second floor and looked down, an unmistakable shudder sweeping his body. He resumed his ascent, stumbled slightly, dragged himself along.

At the moment he reached the third-floor porch, he was rescued. From the gangway along the side of my building, Naka, the woman who lived with my family and looked after me, came running and shrieking. I learned later that she had been sitting in the rear sun parlor of our apartment, knitting placidly, when she saw me plummeting past the window. Thinking I had fallen and would surely have been killed, she ran to the kitchen door. In her frenzy she couldn't get it unlocked and had to run through the house to the front door and race down the stairs and around to the backyard.

Now, catching sight of me in the forefront of the crowd of boys and girls, her shriek of grief turned to relief and then to fury. She called me in a voice the Goddess Hera might have used when she planned a fearful punishment for one of her miscreant children. I left the group and obediently followed her up into the apartment. But even knowing I was going to get whipped couldn't dissipate my triumph.

In the ensuing confusion, Petros beat a retreat. He could blame the appearance of Naka as the reason he hadn't jumped, but everyone knew the truth.

He had escaped, but after that day he never bothered any of us again. He crept through the neighborhood alleys like a fugitive or ghost. If he saw me in time, he crossed a street to avoid me. If we came upon one another unexpectedly, he averted his eyes in a spasm of bewilderment and terror lest I challenge him again to something even more reckless and dangerous. I had gone beyond the boundaries of reason, had challenged him with my life, and he wanted no part of me from that time or forever.

Such was the winter count of a year in my boyhood. So long ago and yet I remember the adventure so clearly. The ways in which this has affected my life are not as clear, although it is a memory I cherish. Then again, I know nothing of the ways it might have affected the life of Petros. Somewhere on this earth, if he's still alive, does he recall now with a tremor of fear and shame what I remember with triumph and jubilation? And what about the hundred boys and girls who were witness to that epic and absurd leap, born of my desperation?

If they remember the event and recount the memory they have of it to others, I wonder, sometimes, if they tell the Homeric tale differently than I have told it now.

The Lesson

WHEN I WAS in my green-boned youth, a little past twelve, we lived in a neighborhood that was a village within the city. Prohibition had just been repealed, the banks had closed, and the country was in the grip of the hungry years.

Looking back from our vantage point today, everything seemed astonishingly cheap. A box of cornflakes cost eight cents, a quart of milk a dime, a dental filling a dollar. Yet inexpensive as everything might have been made little difference because money to buy anything was so scarce.

My father was a Greek Orthodox priest with his parish in a South Side neighborhood. In addition to my mother, there were six children in our family, three boys and three girls. Four siblings were older than I was and a sister was younger. The four oldest worked part-time jobs and contributed to expenses. My sister and I were spared outside employment because of our ages but helped my mother in her housework and by running errands.

For a period of several years, we moved every year. I suspect those moves came because new tenants were allowed the first two month's free rent. Yet each of the apartments we occupied in the three-story buildings had the same bleak, cramped interiors, small bedrooms, and still smaller bathrooms, like cubicles in the labyrinth of Daedalus.

The warmest and most convivial room in the apartment was always the kitchen. There my mother daily replicated the miracle of the loaves and fishes. The Greek rice dish, pilaf, was one of her staples, and she prepared it several times a week in great pots. Yet with culinary cunning she dismembered one scrawny chicken into each pot of pilaf. In her wisdom she understood a morsel of poultry suggested a more wholesome meal. My sister and I, being the youngest, were often left with the less palatable parts of the fowl. But I did not know they were undesirable then and I confess those meals have left me with a propensity for the chicken's tail and neck.

The cloistered neighborhood in which we lived was populated by several ethnic and religious groups. There were Greek Orthodox and Italian Catholics, and Russian and Polish Jews. We lived and played together amicably because poverty compelled us into democracy. How could I harbor any prejudice against a Catholic or Jewish boy whose pants were as ragged as mine?

Little was known of family planning then, so large families were the norm. To clothe the mob of children was an imposing challenge. The only clothing store in our neighborhood was owned by a wily shopkeeper who handled only two sizes. "A perfect fit!" or "He'll grow into it!"

In his emporium, clothing was not displayed on racks but piled in great mounds on several large tables. The piles might include a few new items, but most of the clothing was used. To see a half-dozen mothers foraging through piles to find garments suitable for their offspring could only be compared to an army seeking plunder.

But there was very little cash to pay for store-bought clothing, whether used or new. So an energetic activity of the mothers was the ancient trade of barter.

In this exchange of clothing, my mother was a skillful contestant. She had an intuitive sense about which boys and girls in our block were outgrowing dresses and jackets the quickest and which of these garments could be accommodated to the needs of our family.

It was true that for a good part of the year we wore as little clothing as possible. The boy's attire was a simple pair of pants, T-shirt, socks, and battered sneakers. The girls wore plain dresses or shorts. But as fall began to chill our days, we needed more durable apparel. So the first traces of colder weather compelled a frenzy of haggling. Mothers would visit one another after dinner carrying an armful of clothing. A girl's dress for a boy's shirt. A boy's blazer for a girl's jacket.

In the same way that we tended to be tolerant of one another's ethnicity and religion, we were forbearing of the shabby and mismatched clothing that graced our lithe, young bodies. Clothing was something we wore to keep us decent. From time to time some aberration drew our derision but those taunts passed quickly. That is until the appearance of the green and yellow coat.

So many years have passed since then that I wonder if I am making that coat more appalling than it really was.

Lacking the vocabulary at the time to properly describe the garment, in recalling it now, the words hideous and ghastly come to mind.

The coat first appeared on a late November afternoon worn by my next-door neighbor, Seymour. He was about a year older than I was, ten pounds heavier, with a doleful demeanor. Or perhaps I remember it as doleful because the coat belonged to him.

Seymour emerged from the hallway of his building. A half dozen of us at play in the street fell silent, staring at the approaching apparition. The colors were what struck us first. A sickly green and a pallid yellow. But the colors also seemed to leak into one another so the yellow had traces of green and the green traces of yellow. In the same way, the material was indefinable, suggesting mostly a kind of frayed wool or threadbare fleece. There was also a ragged belt that Seymour wore as if it were a noose.

Seymour witnessed our collective shock and hesitated, as if pondering whether to flee back inside. By then it was too late. Our relentless taunting and mocking had begun.

All through that cold and dismal winter, Seymour wore that coat that was so ugly it offended even our primitive aesthetic senses. But since the coat was also an inanimate object, all our scorn and ridicule was hurled upon the wearer. He would have gladly thrown it away and borne the elements stoically, but his parents warned him somberly that he might fall ill from exposure and die. In the end Seymour endured that winter more wretched than poor Hester

Prynne in the Nathaniel Hawthorne novel we studied in school. Her letter was only scarlet while Seymour's coat was yellow and green.

Finally the worst of winter passed. Then, on a cold day in early March, a coatless Seymour emerged from his apartment, so buoyant and unburdened he might have been naked. Although we had some cold days later in March and in early April, Seymour never wore that coat again.

April cavorted into May and May frolicked into June. The sun grew stronger and we stripped off layers of clothing until we played, almost naked, our arms, legs, and faces growing tanned from the sun.

Yet in that blustery, subzero region known as the Midwest, the sun's reign is transitory. Before we knew it, summer had passed.

As autumn arrived, we prepared for school. The mothers returned like itinerant peddlers to haggling and bartering over clothing.

On a Saturday evening my mother returned from one of her trading sessions. My sisters met her with shrieks at our front door, anxious to see the wardrobe she had assembled for them. I had not given serious attention to what clothing I needed. My mother's vigilant eye took care of that and I trusted in her judgment. That is, until I saw amidst the dresses she had brought for my sisters, the monstrous green and yellow coat she had traded to replace my own worn and outgrown coat.

I pleaded for mercy. At the same time I could not confess to her how we had all tormented poor Seymour. She was a religious lady and might have felt my inheriting the coat was evidence of divine justice. In response to my entreaties, she was sympathetic but also adamant. The coat was all I would have to wear to protect me from the implacable cold of the coming winter.

I had never faced the onslaught of any winter with greater dread than I did that year. I avoided wearing the cursed coat as long as I could. When the weather did finally turn cold I took a circuitous back-alley route to school. A half-block away I removed the coat, bunched it up, and stuffed it into a shopping bag.

In that way I managed to avoid exposure for several weeks. But on a frigid Saturday in early November my mother sent me to the grocery for eggs and bread. Despite my insistence that I'd run both ways, she made me wear the coat.

I purchased the items from the grocery, ignoring the look of pity on the grocer's face. As I emerged from the store I came face-to-face with a cluster of my friends about to enter the store. Seymour was with them.

I was close enough to witness the shock and disbelief on their faces. That turned quickly to sadistic glee. As their raucous taunts began, Seymour stepped forward quickly and aligned himself beside me. Staring defiantly at the jeering mob, he put his arm protectively and reassuringly around my shoulders. That gesture of defense and support from someone who had suffered our taunts through an entire winter startled the others. They could not comprehend such magnanimity of spirit and it awed and silenced them. In an awkward hush, they turned and shuffled away. And in that glowing moment, Seymour and I bonded like comrades. I understood that because of his greatness of soul, I had been spared.

Now, a lifetime later, as I recount this story, I am intemperately moved once again. What befell me then in my twelfth year of life was a lesson in tolerance and forgiveness so searing and unforgettable, it rivaled one of those Greek dramas in which my ancestors portrayed heroes and gods.

Reflections on a
Photograph

I STUDY the 8-by-10-inch, black-and-white photograph given to me by my classmate Harry Pappas at our parochial school reunion. It was taken of our seventh-grade class on November 25, 1936, a little more than sixty years ago.

There are twelve students in the photograph—eight sitting at their desks and four standing—our teacher, Ms. Henrietta, and the principal of our school, Father Constantine, who was also assistant priest to my father in his parish. The unknown photographer had set up the camera in the back of the classroom, and the seated students are twisted around to face the lens.

My younger sister, Irene, who died just a few years ago, is in a front row seat. (We were in the same room because I had fallen a class behind after an illness.) Behind Irene is Leo. Seated in the adjoining row are Polly and Frances. Then there are Ted, Tom, Spero, and Harry, all classmates and playmates, part of our close-knit group, sharing small triumphs and small travails.

I try to imagine what each of them would look like at my age, but it becomes impossible. Their faces are arrested into the youthful images of the photograph. They will always remain that way for me, forever as young as we were in those halcyon days when we played against time in games we always won and had no fear of age and death.

The four students standing are a boy and girl on each side of Ms. Henrietta's desk. I am the boy to her right. Anyone knowing me today would recognize at once the oversized ears. I am tall and skinny (hard to believe I was ever skinny) and wear a long, shapeless sweater with too-short sleeves. Shirt and tie were mandatory dress for the boys, but my tie is askew. My most distinctive accouterment is my safety patrol boy's white belt, which I wear with obvious pride.

Standing next to me is the exquisite Elpe. I'm sure I maneuvered to occupy that treasured place beside her. She wasn't only the seventh-grade beauty but far and away the loveliest girl in the school. Although the black-and-white photograph shows her to be attractive, it does not do her justice.

Elpe was black-haired with a complexion the shade of glistening olives. She had small, shapely ears and a sensuous mouth. A line from a poem of Lord Byron captured her eyes as "belonging in the sun's face . . . imperishably pure beyond all things below." I imagined that the incomparable Helen of Troy, whose beauty launched a thousand ships, must have resembled Elpe.

In the photograph she is wearing not a queen's garment but a simple, sleeveless frock that cannot camouflage her slender, sublime body. Every gesture of her hands and movement of her body radiated a gracefulness that exposed the awkwardness of other girls her age.

I adored Elpe, but so did every other boy in our school. Most of them had handsomer physical attributes than I, and many were better athletes. But I fought for Elpe's favor with my own weapons, a flair for language and a vivid imagination. The happiest part of my school year was acting with Elpe in one of the old Greek tragedies. She played the part of the melancholy princess with such poignancy that people in the audience wept. On another occasion, in a desperate effort to impress her, I told an enormous lie. But that is another story.

Our teacher, Ms. Henrietta, sits at her desk, a comely but unsmiling woman who abhorred any frivolity in the classroom. When I first read about the temperance activist Carry Nation, I thought of Ms. Henrietta. I could easily imagine her demolishing an iniquitous tavern with a bat, while admonishing the patrons to mend their debauched ways. But Ms. Henrietta was also a dedicated teacher who worked valiantly to instill knowledge in our obdurate heads.

Standing with his arm resting on her desk is Father Constantine—small, dapper and dark-haired. His white clerical collar rings his throat like a noose. His favorite means of discipline was the liberal use of a stout wooden rod that he carried with him as other men carried watches and combs. For some baffling reason, he spent an inordinate amount of time watching me; and as a result, I suffered the cursed rod for numerous infractions. Yet in later years I freely acknowledged my debt to him in so many ways. When he died a year ago, I was among several former students who eulogized him.

Standing to the left of Ms. Henrietta is another attractive girl whose name eludes me now. Perhaps her identity is obscured by her proximity to Elpe. Beside this unidentified girl stands George, a handsome, dark, curly-haired youth with a lean athletic body and an engaging smile. He also wears a white patrol boy's belt. Even as I longed for Elpe to love me, I felt then she deserved someone as heroic as George. I could be unselfish about him because in the entire school George was my closest friend. It is about him that I wish to write now.

As a beginning, I must confess that George was a poor student. He sat at a desk in the rear of the room, striving to remain as unobtrusive as possible. For the most part he succeeded. But when Ms. Henrietta finally remembered him and called on him for a response to her question, his anguish was visible. He rose slowly and unhappily to his feet and stood mutely beside his desk, sweeping his hand nervously through his hair. If Ms. Henrietta felt merciless, she would keep him standing. If she felt merciful, she would allow him to sit down. Because he was my friend, I suffered his anguish and always breathed a sigh of relief when he was finally back in the sanctuary of his seat.

But at recess or after school, George came into his glory. We saw what our teacher could not see, the superb way he could run, jump, bat and fight. He was the strongest and fleetest among us, the best athlete in the school, whatever the sport. What the rest of us struggled to do, George accomplished effortlessly. At the same time he was also a born leader, with a quality of dignity that superseded all his anguished muteness in the classroom.

In our perpetual warfare with the young black Catholics in the Roman Catholic parish school across the street, George was our captain. His prowess was respected and feared by our antagonists, and yet he was also the one who sought to deliver us from our intolerance and bigotry. He met several times with the young black leaders in an effort to achieve an armistice. These uneasy truces lasted for a short while until passion and fear prevailed once more and peace broke down. The unhappy result was that through most of our school year a state of racial and religious war existed between our parish schools. When fighting with fists and stones erupted, George put aside the cloak of peacemaker and led us in our battles, as many centuries earlier a warrior named Achilles commanded another army of Greeks.

In addition to being courageous, George also could be trusted to equitably settle any of our disputes. He seemed to have an innate sense of justice and fairness. When the rest of us argued, his decision was accepted as final. He also set a scrupulous standard of moral conduct. This was brought painfully home to me on one occasion when a small group of us teased a frailer, more timid classmate in the schoolyard. I had not taken the initiative, but I eagerly joined the tormentors, gleeful as the rest of them when the poor victim broke down in tears.

At that moment, our little band of hoodlums was struck by an avenging fury. George pounced upon us, slapping heads and kicking behinds. After the others stumbled and scattered, he turned to me. Secure in our friendship I made no effort to flee. I smiled, a smile that was shattered when he struck me a stunning blow across the head. I was catapulted to the ground, a cry of pain bursting from my lips. I stared up at him in shock and disbelief, not only because he had struck me, but because he had hit me harder than he had hit any of the others. He must have grasped my unspoken question.

"Because you should have known better," he said quietly.

I understood the extent of my transgression then and felt the pangs of remorse more than I felt the pain of his blow.

Sometimes on balmy spring or summer evenings, a group of boys including George and me would walk to the lake. We would sit on the rocks and stare out across the water at the tankers and freighters journeying to distant ports. One of the games we played was to call out the name of a far-off, exotic city where we planned someday to travel. "Singapore," one would say. "Hong Kong," said another. "Babylon," said a third—and we mocked him for confusing Bible studies with real geography. My own contribution, delivered slowly, my tongue lavishing great care on each syllable, was "Vla-di-vos-tok." I had only the vaguest notion where that city was located, but that did not matter, because it had the desired effect of intimidating my companions.

I can never recall George naming a city. We did not think much of it at the time, accepting that he was no more proficient in geography than he was in any other subject.

But I think now George simply could not envision what a part of him understood he would never see.

That summer when we completed seventh grade, we looked for work. Our families were submerged in the Depression, and if we could not find a way to earn a little money, our pockets remained empty.

George had been working after school in a neighborhood grocery, and through his efforts I was also hired to stack the fruit and bag the vegetables. The owner of the grocery, a gravel-voiced immigrant from the renowned city of Sparta in Greece sought to make us aware of the resonances of history that existed, as well, in the confines of his shabby store. He sold the same delectable cheeses and olives that once had been served to Alexander the Great and his generals. Wines from the islands of Samos and Santorini he stored on his shelves were the same wines that had graced the celebrant tables of the kings of Sparta and Thebes. In spite of the grocer's impassioned lectures, those hours I spent each afternoon with George made for one of the most joyful summers of my youth.

After I graduated from parochial school, my family sent me downstate to Urbana to attend high school and live with my brother Mike, who was studying at the University of Illinois. During the months I spent away, I wrote George several times. He was a poor correspondent and never answered my letters. After a while I did not write again.

When I was home for Christmas, I visited George at the grocery, where he still worked. He was attending high school, suffering with his studies, in constant danger of flunking. The months of separation had produced a certain awkwardness between us, and while we pledged to get together, I left without seeing George again.

When I returned to Chicago the following summer, George's family had moved out of our neighborhood. I made a halfhearted effort to locate him and then gave up.

For the following two years I did not see George. War had broken out in Europe with the Nazi invasion of Poland. When I gathered with boys my own age, we talked of America entering the war. We were excited at the prospect of becoming soldiers, and yet anxious whether we would measure up to the task of bravely serving our country. The only youth those who knew him agreed would make a courageous soldier was George.

Later that summer, running by chance into a classmate who had seen George not long before, I learned he had dropped out of high school. The last my classmate heard, George was working in another grocery, at Western Avenue and Roosevelt Road.

I was suddenly nostalgic to see my friend again, and I rode a streetcar west to that neighborhood. I located the grocery, where a clerk told me George wasn't working there. The clerk had been employed only a few months, and he suggested I wait to speak to the owner, who would return later in the day. I decided to wait for him.

The owner returned at twilight and was busy for a little while, so we could not speak. When he finally had a moment, in response to my question, he told me George was dead.

At first I didn't believe him, certain he had made a mistake, that we were not speaking about the same person.

But he went on to describe the George I remembered and also told me how he had died. He had scratched his hand on a rusty nail and the scratch became infected. George died of tetanus—a disease that as children we called lockjaw.

I don't remember how I got home that night, what streetcar I rode, how long it took to cross the city. I kept seeing images of George running or leaping, brimming with vigor and with life. Although I had experienced the deaths of old parishioners in my father's parish, they seemed ancient relics to whom death came in its proper time. I did not understand how someone who seemed so invincible could die. I was young then, it is true, and not yet aware that the moment we are born, we are old enough to die.

In the following few years, through the turmoil and chaos of war, all over the world men and women of all ages were dying. The grocer's story and George's death were obscured in that throng.

Shortly after the war ended, at our parish church in a gathering that included several former classmates, someone brought up George's name. None of the others knew what had happened to him.

I'm not sure just what drove me to deceive them then. I can't even remember if I sought to hedge my words by saying it was only what I had heard, but I recounted my story as if it contained the blazing conviction of truth. I told them that when the war broke out, George volunteered for the army. He proved an exceptional soldier and was commissioned a lieutenant. He was sent overseas, I continued, and fought in a series of battles which earned him decorations.

In one of the final battles of the war, George had been killed.

Those students who remembered George's exploits in the schoolyard and on the athletic field easily believed the story to be true.

In the years that followed, caught up in the entanglements of my own life, I rarely thought of George. When I did, it was mostly on those occasions when I watched a superb athlete perform on a baseball diamond or basketball court.

Then, some twenty years after the war, at a reunion of our parish school, a classmate I had not seen since graduation asked me if I had heard what had happened to George. Before I had a chance to answer, he besieged me with a story of George dying heroically in the war while carrying wounded comrades to safety through a fierce enemy barrage.

My classmate's recital was much more elaborate and dramatic than the story I had told years earlier. For a bewildered moment, defying reason, I considered he was telling me the truth. Then I understood his story was simply the one I first told, enlarged and enhanced through numerous recountings, adorned with the flourishes of time and the trappings of myth.

Now, holding the class photograph in my hands, the memories of that springtime of my life return. I see us as we were then—at play in the fields of innocence. When we looked on things with our clear, young eyes, we could not know how blind was our vision and how little we truly saw.

If I fabricated a story about the destiny of George, it

was because he was my friend and I loved him. A friend has the responsibility to be a witness. I had witnessed George's prowess, the aura of invincibility around him, and that made it easy for me to create a story about what I truly believed would have transpired if George had lived.

As for what happened to my story. . . . When we have spent enough years on earth and gained knowledge of the longings that exist within us and in the hearts of others, we may finally understand that if there is anything truer than truth, it is the legend with which we frail mortals embellish that truth.

The Horse Gamblers

▨▨▨ WHEN I WAS a year from twenty and two years before I married, seeking the who, the what, and the how of
the action, I began gambling. Rationalizing my infatuation,
I sagely observed that all life was a wheel of fortune. When
one entered a plane or car, speculated in the market, joined
in the jousts of politics and war, and, particularly, when one
staked a tender, brooding heart on the guile and duplicity of
a pretty girl, the fickleness of chance bedeviled all.

I played poker, rolled craps, and hit or stood at 21. But
my first love was the horses. Betting them singly or in parlays, with the meticulous dedication of an accountant, I
charted them by weight, class, distance, time of workout,
and jockey. Since my only memories of steeds were the poor
spavined creatures hauling milk wagons through the city alleys, my true interest, so I reasoned, was not in noble animals engaging in the sport of kings. Like Starbuck, who
could not see why Ahab should go whaling for anything
but profit, I was aghast that anyone might gamble indiffer-
ent to winning. Since the dream of every American youth
was to become a millionaire, I would make my million gambling.

During this period, which lasted several years, my day began about 10:30 in the morning when the ringing of the doorbell in my father's house would intrude into my sleep. Naka, the old and faithful guardian of our hearth, would answer and reluctantly admit my friend Chris Reed. He was a year older than I, an animated and charming fellow with a penchant for the racing form. He would invade my bedroom crying, "They're off!" raising the shade on my protesting eyes. While I washed and dressed, he sat on the edge of the tub, briefing me on the prospects of horses at various tracks. When we prepared to leave, Chris gallantly attempting to kiss Naka's hand, she warned him balefully to cease his disreputable influence on younger boys.

Walking the two blocks to the neighborhood handbook on 63rd Street, Chris had his racing form rolled tightly and jammed under his arm.

"Marion's Boy is going again at Tropical," Chris said.

"I marked him down for a bet."

"And Sally's Pal in the first at Belmont. Remember how he closed in the stretch last time? Old Teddy Atkinson is on him today."

"Then he won't be more than two or three to one."

"But a good omen to start the day with a winner," Chris said. "I feel this is going to be the day!"

"You say that every day."

"I know! I know!" Chris laughed. "But today will be different!"

We turned down an alley, walking beneath the elevated tracks, a train passing above us with a roar, breaking the sun into a checkerboard of flashing light and shade. Entering a warehouse, we climbed a flight of stairs to a door. We knocked and a peephole slid open.

"It's the Lone Ranger and Tonto," Chris said.

The door was opened and we entered.

"Today is the day, friend!" Chris announced buoyantly to the satrap guarding the door. "By this evening you may be working for me!"

Shrugging off the doorman's grunt, we passed along a corridor leading into a large, bare-floored but brightly lit hall. Later in the day, as racing began at tracks around the country, the hall would be filled with true believers obeying St. Paul's exhortation to glory in tribulation. But in the morning when Chris and I entered, only a handful of sports were present, standing before the track charts tacked on the walls.

Greeting a few people along the way, waving amiably to Hymie sitting at the teller's window, Chris and I moved to a few chairs in a corner we reserved for our small contingent. The only other person already there was Gero Kampana.

He was an ancient Greek, perhaps as old as ninety. A porter from a nearby barbershop brought him to the handbook early in the morning and picked him up again at night to take him to whatever room he slept in. All day he sat in his chair, a withered, white-haired specter, eyes receded into the hollows of his skull, his flesh wasted and webbed. The legend they told about him was that for almost all of his life he had gambled. He had never married, never loved a woman, never traveled farther than the boundaries of the nearest track or card room. Playing until his faculties dimmed and failed, he could neither see nor hear well any more, and he rarely spoke except for an occasional whisper when he asked one of us to make a bet for him or bring him a carton of soup or coffee. But he could not bear to be separated from his passion, and later in the day when the crowd in the hall would grow frenzied and shrill, the excitement at its peak, he would begin to tremble, absorbing the rhythm and odors of the surgings and steamings around him.

In the next hour we were joined by Sarnis, a sixtyish short-order cook in a nearby lunchroom; he exuded a stale odor of spent coffee grounds and grease. Milton, a bread truck driver who once had stepped on a horse turd in an alley and later that day won a $900 parlay. Forever after, his route to the handbook was taken through alleys. And, finally, Leahy, a steelworker and one-time wrestler who dreamed of breeding thoroughbreds in one of Ireland's greener counties.

We were drawn together by the need to share the excitement of the action. Even Gero Kampana, solitary and friendless as a dying wolf, shunned sitting alone. For part of the thrill of gambling came when a man could lament his losing to sympathetic ears or boast of his boldness and skill as the reasons he had won. While in the hours we had spent together, there had grown between us the camaraderie of athletes, warming up, taking their adversaries' measure.

"Did you fellows see Marion's Boy is going again?" Sarnis asked.

"I put the nag in all my parlays," Leahy said. "Best bet of the day."

"Not as good a bet as Sally's Pal in the opener at Belmont," Chris said. "That sweetheart will kiss off my glorious day."

"I'm betting Modesto in that race," I said. "He's got an edge on class."

"You're crazy, boy!" Chris cried. "Sally's Pal will whip his ass! Especially with Atkinson the Ace riding!"

"I'm not so sure about that," Milton said.

"That's the difference between you turkeys and me," Chris winked. "You're not sure, but I know."

"A gambler don't know nothing," Sarnis said gloomily. "If he did, he'd be living in a big house in Florida, with flunkies and lots of girls, making one big play a month."

A whistle of breath came from Gero Kampana's withered lips. We looked at him, but none of us could be sure whether he heard and agreed with what Sarnis had said.

By the time the first race of the day at Belmont Park was about to run, the hall was nearly full. Conductors from the railroad, housewives, waiters and porters, peddlers and ladies of the evening, all shoved and hurried to the tellers' windows where Hymie had been joined by a band of ticket writers dressed, like a chorus of Rockettes, in expensive silk shirts and finely tailored gabardine jackets. They wrote tickets swiftly, brusquely hollered "next!" and were careful not to graze the fingers or sleeves of any of the shabby patrons on the outside of the grills.

Clutching the small slips that receipted our wagers, we gathered beneath the loudspeaker hanging in the corner. When the droning voice of the wire-service announcer notified us the horses were at the post, the crowd surged forward, bunching more tightly.

"They're off at Belmont!"

Silent and alert for the first call, we stared up at the loudspeaker like an enraptured congregation awaiting an evangelist's words.

"At the quarter, Double Jay by a length, Dolphin second by two lengths, Sally's Pal running third."

"Come on, Sally's Pal!" Chris cried. "Come on, baby, bless my day!"

Around us, others murmured or chanted their prayers and pleas.

"At the half, Double Jay by a head, Dolphin second by a length, Sally's Pal running third. On the outside, With Wings is running fourth."

"Atkinson is making his move!" Chris said.

"Come on, Double Jay!" a woman near us called.

"I'm sorry for you, lady, very sorry," Chris grinned. "I think your nag is dying."

"In the stretch, Dolphin by half a length, Sally's Pal second by a length, With Wings running third."

"Shit," the woman said.

"Come on, baby," Chris pleaded. "Come on, my sweetheart."

Since my horse, Modesto, had not yet received a call, I joined Chris in his plea.

"Come on, Sally's Pal!" I cried.

From the stretch call to the announcement of the winner was always the longest and most agonizing interval of the race.

"At Belmont, in the first race, the winner is With Wings . . . Sally's Pal second . . . Dolphin third."

"Shit, shit," the woman said.

Chris groaned loudly and stared with disbelief at the loudspeaker.

"He must have been nipped at the wire," I said consolingly. "I bet it was a photo."

"I told you guys what I thought of Sally's Pal," Milton said smugly.

"Did your horseshit even get a call?" Chris asked mockingly.

Milton silently extended his stub showing three dollars bet on the winner.

Chris and I hooted and pounded Milton's back. Accepting the acclaim, he finally shook us off and with a proud and stately stride made his way through the crowd toward the cashier's window to await the posting of the price the winner paid.

"A horse is a horse," Sarnis said sadly as he tore up his ticket. "Some days they want to run and some days they feel like dying."

But there was little time for post mortems. Another track began its races and there were other bets to be made. By the middle of the afternoon, six tracks going off at erratic intervals, the rushing and tumult became pandemonium. The floor was littered with torn and discarded tickets, men and women rushing to the tellers as another race went to the post. A suffocating stench swept the hall: sweat and tension, jubilation and terror, hope and desperation.

Returning to our chairs to rest for a few moments, Chris motioned at Gero Kampana and grimaced.

"He's gone in his pants again."

"Poor old devil," I said.

Chris stared at the old man for a long moment, not a cruel or insensitive look, simply a bewildered and pitying one.

"What keeps him alive?" he asked me softly. "What brings him here day after day and keeps him alive?"

"I don't know," I said.

The old man seemed to look beyond us, his head inclined toward the tumult of the crowd.

"I'd kill myself before I lived like that," Chris said.

By late afternoon, many of the players had given up or been driven away. A few who remained were winners, doggedly pushing to increase their winnings. Many were losers, making a final effort to redeem their day. For until the final race had been run, the last horse crossing the wire, hope beat in any good gambler's heart.

I suppose most of us who lingered to the end feared, above all, not being able to play at all. Time spent away from the action found us restless and bored. More important than a happy birth, a safe voyage, or a good harvest, we yearned to keep the spheres of our planet whirling.

Sometimes in the waning of the afternoon, immersed in the warmth and fervor of the crowd, I'd catch Chris's eye and we'd smile, winking like conspirators, nourished by the knowledge we were friends riding the same wild comet.

For almost three years, that was about the way I spent my days. In the evenings I worked a few hours at a neighborhood liquor store and dated a childhood sweetheart for dinner and a show. We were married in that time and with my nuptial vows I promised to forsake my other passion. My wife helped, but our resolutions faded before the restlessness that started in me as the first of the day's races would begin to run. I started gambling again, accepting certain alterations. Instead of Chris picking me up at home, the two of us facing the censure and distress of my wife, we met in the handbook.

In that time there was a morning when old Gero Kampana was not in his chair. Hymie told us the porter said he had died in his sleep. We talked about him for a day or two, feeling some obligation to send a small wreath because he sat with us. But nobody knew where the old man lived or cared enough to find the porter. After a while we did not mention the old man again and no one mourned his passing.

By the end of those three years, our little group had disbanded. Plagued by arthritis, Sarnis moved to Florida, working as a short-order cook in a lunchroom not far from Tropical Park. Milton's brother-in-law died of a stroke, and he moved to Baltimore to help his sister run a small family grocery. We had a Christmas card from him once and then did not hear from him again. Leahy married a widow with four small children, acquiring an instant family. Working hard to keep them fed and clothed, after a while he stopped coming to the handbook. Visiting him at his home one night, Chris and I found him in the basement shining his children's shoes, the varied sizes lined up in a neat, glistening row, each shoe taking him one step further from his dream of breeding horses in Ireland.

Chris and I were the last to separate. The decision was

mine since I could no longer fool myself into believing the gambling was laughter and pleasure any longer. Somewhere along the way, like the prophecy of Teiresias, "He that came seeing, blind shall he go," I lost restraint and control. One terrifying night I gambled away the money my father had given me from his own meager salary to pay my rent. My wife was pregnant then and her anguished question, "Haven't we suffered enough?" seemed finally to permit no other answer. In this time of emptiness and the pangs of withdrawal, I turned back to the writing I had wanted to do since childhood.

Chris and I pledged fervently to keep in touch, but our paths ran separately and that wasn't possible. After several months, driving down 63rd Street, I saw him walking toward the alley entrance to the handbook, the racing form rolled tightly and jammed under his arm. I honked my horn and he turned back and came to where I parked.

"How you doing, sport?" I asked.

"Fine," he said. "Fine. How's married life?"

"Like racing," I said. "You win some and lose some."

He grinned and nodded.

"Picking many winners?" I asked.

"You know me, kid," he said. "Every race is a new adventure."

We were both silent for a moment.

"I gotta go," he said. "The first at Belmont will be running soon and I got a beauty to kiss the beginning of my day."

"Good luck, sport," I said.

"Stay out in front," he said.

After that morning I did not see Chris for almost thirty years. I thought of him a few times when I was writing a story of races or cards, and for a few moments, memory returned the emotion of those intemperate days.

Until a morning a couple of years ago, sitting in the Northwestern Station, waiting for a train to take me to a suburban college for a lecture, I heard the announcement of a race train leaving for Arlington Park. A group of men and women rose from the surrounding benches and started toward the gate. One of the men tightly rolled the form he had been reading and jammed it under his arm. There was something familiar in the gesture and something recognizable about his height and stance. As he came closer I started to call his name and then I saw his face. For a shaken moment it recalled another face, wasted by a single passion, consumed by a solitary intensity that locked out all the world.

I did not speak and then he was gone, disappearing through the gate toward the train.

I have thought of that moment a number of times since then. I could have been mistaken; it was not Chris, but a much older man resembling the buoyant friend I remembered. Yet I cannot fool myself for long, because I know the man was Chris. By the spinnings of chance and the vagaries of fate that helped me free myself, he had remained imprisoned, until like the old gambler Gero Kampana, he had looked too long into the fire.

Show me a gambler, the old cook Sarnis would say, and I'll tell you a sad story. Perhaps that is true, but life is full of sad stories. Survival is a precarious balancing on the brink of varied disasters. But, having looked into that fire myself, I think a special prayer is needed for those who live in a world where time means nothing and noon and midnight pass unnoticed.

In the end, whatever our prisons and our sufferings, there is, after all, an ultimate consolation. They can last only a lifetime, and eventually, inevitably, death frees us once again.

The Warmth of
Halsted Street

AFTER AN ABSENCE of almost six months from the Attic haunts of Halsted Street, I returned recently to collect impressions and refresh memories.

Although the world around us changes with each day's news, the few blocks of Halsted just southwest of the Loop seem to survive unchanged. Like a shabby movie set for a neighborhood fallen on hard times, the structures look worn and battered, rows of drab, narrow stores set between bright, glittering restaurants. In the last few years, new restaurants—the Roditys, the Greek Islands, and Dianna's Opaa—have joined the Hellas, the Grecian Gardens, the Diana Grocery and Restaurant, and the Parthenon; the fervor for Greek food and wine in an ebullient atmosphere provides adequate commerce for all. Not only have these establishments escaped demolition and survived the building of the University of Illinois complex, but they thrive, drawing many of the students as patrons.

I start at the corner of Halsted and Jackson with a brief call at the Athenian Candle Company, whose windows are decorated with candles of varied colors and sizes and icons of the Madonna, Jesus, and saints. The atmosphere, redolent with scents of incense and wax, always evokes for me the gilded churches of my childhood, a time of innocence and untroubled faith. Closing my eyes, I can recall the luminous figure of my father in the portal of the sanctuary, clad in his vestments, holding the chalice of communion above his head. Then I visit with Sam and Angela Godelas, gentle people who preside like an engaging lord and lady over their sanctified domain.

Leaving them, I walk a few steps to the Mandakas Jewelry shop, operated by Helen Mandakas, an attractive, gray-haired widow respected and liked by everyone. Her small shop is a storehouse of information about the street, the marriages and deaths, the failures and successes.

I have never entered the archaic barbershop nearby because the barber might think I want a haircut, but passing his window I pause each time because of the chipped plaster bust that stands just inside the glass: a statue of the hero of the Greek War of Independence in 1821, Theodore Kolokotrones, his fierce, hawklike visage under the great plumed war helmet he wore in battle staring sternly across the turmoil of the street. During the long years of exile he spent on Zante, he would take his sons to the peak of the castle hill, point across the Ionian Sea to the mountains of the Morea, where he was born, and talk of his dream of returning there to help free Greece from the Turks. That was a dream the old general helped his country achieve thru ten long, terrible years of war.

The Mediterranean Pastry Shop is a bright, clean little

store sold not long ago to a pair of enterprising young men, Mike Lembidakis and Stratos Taoultsides. Mike is a Cretan who adds an extra measure of gusto to his greeting when he hears my parents are also from Crete. I linger longingly before trays of succulent pastries, the delicate, shell-like diples, the honey-glutted baklava, from time to time casting a quick, admiring glance at the young Greek girl behind the counter whose comeliness, like the dark flowers of a poet's love lyric, ornaments that glen where tiny frosted nymphs stand poised on the escarpment of cakes.

At twilight I pass one of several bare-walled, bleak coffeehouses that remain in the neighborhood, the same old Greek men like an assemblage of withered ganders, peacocks, toms, rams, and bullocks scattered among the clothless tables. Some sip small cups of Greek coffee, reading Greek newspapers. Others simply stare into the whorls of smoke curling about their heads. They cannot really be the same men I have seen at these tables for so many years. Death must have taken many of them, and others have slipped into their places. But they appear the same to me, gaunt monks cloistered in those austere cells, without curiosity any longer about the world outside, emptied of futile longings, drained of vain ambitions, as if they have come to understand the truth of Parmenides: that human experience is just the shadow of a dream having nothing to do with the way things really are.

When I enter Acropolis Imports, Meletis Roussos comes vibrantly to greet me; his handsome wife, Maria, waves from the office in the rear. The store is full of copper kettles and statues, linens and weavings, all imported from

Greece, and includes one of the best collections of Greek records and tapes in the city.

Meletis, a stocky, strong man, swarthy as a Moor, has a deep, resonant voice that almost sings. Indeed, singing has been his profession: he has performed with the Royal Opera Company in Rome and the San Carlos Opera Company in Napoli. I have always thought that kings like Oedipus and Agamemnon would have had voices like the voice of Meletis Roussos.

We speak of journeys we have both made in the past few years to Greece. Before I leave, he gives me a recently recorded album on which he sings heroic songs of Greece, and he signs the jacket with a flourish. (I play that record now as I write, his bass-baritone voice vibrating richly in my ears.)

Growing hungry, I am drawn by the browned lamb turning slowly on a spit in the window of the Parthenon. Chris Liakouras greets me, takes me to a table, and bread, cheese, olives, and wine appear quickly as a prelude to my dinner. I watch the waiters carrying trays as heavy as Ajax's shield, moving swiftly, joking with the customers, expounding like Sophists on the menu.

"That is stuffed grape leaves in sauce."

"Is it good?"

"All Greek food is good!"

"Is it good here?"

"Here it is the best of all!"

Under the pressure of their expanding business, Chris and his brother Bill have added a second large room to the Parthenon. They are smiling and friendly hosts, without the effervescent shouts and hugs one feels inclined to expect of Greeks since Zorba.

As the wine and food stream thru me, I imagine I am sitting in one of the restaurants of Athens late at night, when even the spirited Athenians pause finally to eat. The babble of voices, the shrill clatter of silver and glassware, the mellifluent sentences in Greek, words flying up like startled birds, are the same. The dark-haired waiters look like the same young men from the villages of Greece, working the restaurants in Athens as way stations on their journeys to Australia and America. And the savory fragrance of lamb and veal, sharpened with oregano and lemon, weaves the same sorcery in my nostrils. Alas, when I rise finally to leave and pass into the street, the illusion of Athens succumbs to the harsh reality of Chicago weather.

On the second night I begin at the new Dianna's, where I am met by Petros Kogeones. But it's a Petros I have never seen before. Banished are the ordinary white shirt and dark trousers he wore in the Diana (also owned by Petros and his two brothers). He has replaced them with a resplendent turtleneck sweater and a dazzling sportcoat. Awed, I tell him I am reminded of Saturday afternoons with film people in Beverly Hills. I also remind him that the last time I was there, the restaurant had not yet been opened. He had brought me in to see it, silent then and cluttered with carpenters' ladders and painters' scaffolding. He makes a gesture, a characteristic Greek raising of his brows and flexing of his fingers suggesting that a matchless experience is before me. And he is right.

As the tables fill, Petros is the garrulous, exuberant

host, laughing as he greets a party, beckoning to a waiter as he seats them. On his way back to his station by the door, he sternly disperses a group of waiters who had clustered together. Winking at me, he says with a grin, "To prevent a coup, any assembly of more than three waiters is forbidden!"

Later in the evening, after his patrons have been warmed by the torches of numerous platters of saganaki, to which they shout a jubilant "Opaaaaaaa!" Petros walks among the tables and makes his spiel with the ease of a born Greek pitchman.

"I was born shy," Petros cries to the gathering, which is composed of many students and well-dressed older people. "That's why I can tell you the food here is delicious . . . if you don't think so, get out!"

The patrons clap and laugh in approval, relishing his friendly abuse, perhaps because they know he enjoys and identifies with them.

Afterwards, at a table on a platform in the rear of the big, warm room, a group of girls celebrates a birthday. Under Petros's direction, a file of waiters marches to the table, singing happy birthday and carrying a single tall candle stuck into the neck of a wine bottle.

The Diana Grocery and Restaurant has always held a special place for me, and I keep it for the end of that evening. Peter Kogeones (who stole a scene from Anthony Quinn in "A Dream of Kings") welcomes me as if I were a relative who had been away for years, hugs me vigorously, kisses me on both cheeks, then hurries me to a table with a determination that permits no opposition. With the first glasses of brandy we toast all of Peter's considerable enthusiasms—God, America, Greece, the heroic dead, his father, my books, Agnew (he once ate avgolemono soup in the Diana). While we talk he calls a greeting to all who enter the restaurant, warm thanks and farewell to all who leave, meanwhile enacting a scene we have played many times before.

"Paul, bring uncle here a little lamb!"

"I just ate, Peter. Down the street with Petros."

"You will have some lamb here!"

The waiter brings a plate with half a dozen moist, tender slices of braised lamb, another plate of tomatoes, cucumbers and cheese sprinkled with oil and oregano, a rack of bread, a bottle of wine. I stare at the feast with dismay.

"Peter!" I plead. "I have just eaten!"

"Not a word!" he cries. "You must eat something with me!"

As if to avoid further protests, he leaps up and shakes hands vigorously with several departing patrons.

"Thank you! Come again! Hurry back! God bless America and you too!"

When I finally rise, wobbling under my load of food and wine, he gazes sternly at the half-eaten remnants on my plates. Then, to assure me he is not really angry, he grabs me roughly and hugs me once more.

Passing thru the grocery, I meet Ted Kogeones, another of the brothers. Ted is auburn-haired and mustached, as tall and majestically sinewed as a warrior from some classical frieze. Ted was the wildest and most ebullient of the brothers, until a serious illness struck him some years ago. Altho he has fully recovered, there is a quietness to his demeanor now, a shadow of mortality lingering in his eyes. We embrace, and he looks at me probingly.

"Are you well?"

"I am well, Ted, except I am growing older too fast."

"Hush!" he reproves me softly. "Not a word!" As if by refraining to speak of my years, the gods might overlook them. Then, in his parting smile and the clasp of his strong hands, he adds his pledge of friendship and affection.

Peter follows me turbulently to the door, at the last minute thrusting a bottle of wine under my arm, threatening indescribable mayhem if I wait too long for another visit. I wave them a fond good-by.

On Halsted it is late; a chilled, cold mist has settled across the night, causing me to shiver and tug my coat collar about my ears. For a moment I consider stopping in the Hellas to see the last show, envisioning the singers and dancers I have always enjoyed. But I am sodden and stuffed, and the Hellas must wait, as the Roditys and Greek Islands and Grecian Gardens must, for other nights.

Crossing the street, I walk beside the dark, gloomy buildings standing in silent tiers with parapets of stone and fire escapes of iron. At the corner, unlocking my car, I stand at a curiously encompassing vantage point that allows a full view of the streets from the Grecian Gardens on the south to the new Dianna on the north. Between those garish outposts, glittering and ghostly in the haze, the neighborhood seems a broken, dismal preserve of spurious grandeurs.

Caught by a surge of melancholy, I have a somber vision of the hosts and waiters as sad, fragmented relics of a proud and ancient race, expending their lives under the glow of artificial lights, beside paintings of temples in pallid murals, uncorking bottles of wine instead of launching their ships on Homer's wine-dark sea.

At that moment several groups emerge from a couple of the restaurants. Fortified against the bleakness of the night, they cavort and laugh, singing snatches of Greek melodies, the tumult of their voices echoing loudly and jubilantly as they scatter to their cars. A silence descends upon the street once more. Yet their festive passage has lightened my gloom.

There is a word in Greek, *filotimo*, a word difficult to translate because it involves a feeling one has for strangers, a veneration for visitors and guests. Once, a stranger walking thru a poor village in Greece, I was greeted and taken into every house, offered food from the meager fare, made to feel welcome.

Now, in an instant of altered vision, I think of my friends in the restaurants of Halsted Street as simply extending that *filotimo* beyond their homes. Without Troys or Marathons to engage their energies, without relinquishing their freedom or their pride, they have established small encampments where armies of young people can assemble, expectant and hungry, while lean-hipped and white-aproned Apollos carry them platters of gyros, saganaki, barbecued lamb, and suckling pig, the formidable salads, moussaka, pastitsio, and the wines of Samos, Attica, and Crete. Then, for a little while, in a sanctuary free of moderation and restraint, all celebrate some triumph of that Greek tradition and spirit, that miraculous thrust to joy and to life.

In that moment I offer each of them, the servers and the served, Pindar's prayer for the contestants in a race: "Grant them with feet so light to pass thru life."

Thus, singing under my breath, I enter my car, no longer merely an aging scribe, a squeaker of words, but a redoubtable Odysseus, fearlessly foreshadowing dangers to be met and overcome. Turning the helm of my craft, pointing it along the flexuous trail of night, back to my Ithaca, my hearth, my family and my home. . . .

A Greek Restaurant Man's
Final Page

HE WAS related to my mother, but the precise association has been lost in the recesses of time. I hadn't thought of him for many years until the other day when his goddaughter phoned to tell me he had died in the Veterans Administration Medical Center in North Chicago at the age of ninety-eight. For the following few days I found the embers of old memories shaken.

He was born John Katsoulakis, later shortened to Catsulis, in Lastros Village, Sitia, on the island of Crete in 1888. He came to the United States as a youth, beginning as a dishwasher in restaurant kitchens. During World War I he served at the Great Lakes Naval Station as a baker and cook. For the following sixty-five years he continued working in restaurants in Chicago and Waukegan.

My childhood memories of him evoke a short, strong-bodied, balding man who'd greet my mother and me with ebullience and warmth when we visited his restaurant. We'd sit at a table or in a booth and he'd bring me an immense slice of homemade peach, blueberry, or cherry pie with a glass of milk. That was the auspicious part of the visit for me, since he and my mother conversed on matters I didn't find important. As I grew older, I visited him a few times alone. The pies were just as delicious and a concession to my growth allowed me coffee instead of milk.

In moments when his trade was slack, he sat with me and we talked of my aspirations to write. In encouraging me and discussing my future, he spoke of his past, his first years washing dishes while he struggled to learn English.

"I didn't have an education," he told me, "and wasn't any smarter or any more ambitious than thousands of other immigrants. I was strong, though, and what I could do was work hard. I vowed that if the Irish immigrant worked fourteen hours a day, I'd work sixteen. If the Italian immigrant worked eighteen hours a day, I'd work twenty. And if the German immigrant worked twenty-two hours a day, I'd work twenty-four. That was how I saved money and bought an interest in my first lunchroom."

I recall asking him how anyone could work twenty-four hours a day and not allow time for eating and sleeping.

"A restaurant man learns to eat on his feet," he laughed. "As for sleeping, I'd nap in a chair in the kitchen for a few minutes at a time and wake up when the bell on the front door rang. In the beginning it was hard, but I found even after I could afford help in my lunchroom that I needed only a few hours' sleep a night."

He'd talk, sometimes, of the wonder of his odyssey from Crete to the new land.

"Those of you born here can never understand what this country meant to us," he said. "I remember elders in my village reading aloud letters from relatives over here. There were complaints of loneliness, but most often the letters were full of gratitude and praise for this land. The first word in English I learned to speak in Crete was 'Am-me-ri-ca.' I'd say it in the morning and say it at night before I went to sleep. 'Am-me-ri-ca.' " He spoke the word slowly, lingering over the syllables, making it sound like a song or a poem.

John Catsulis sold one restaurant and bought another in a different location. I lost track of him until, when my first story was published, my mother located him, and I went to show him a copy of the magazine. He inspected it with pleasure and reverence.

"See what I've always told you?" he said. "Could such a wonderful thing take place anywhere but in Am-me-ri-ca?"

I made a retort about writers being published for the first time in other countries as well, but he was unwilling or unable to accept that as true. He hadn't any knowledge of other countries.

"Remember what I tell you," he said. "If those other writers write ten hours a day, you write twelve. If they write fourteen hours a day, you write sixteen. You'll make it all right then."

Years passed once more when I didn't see him. I didn't feel any urgency to visit him, perhaps wearied by his unrelenting litany of work. I knew he was a kind and generous man because my mother told me he sent a great deal of money back to Crete to help his nephews and nieces through school and to bring some of them to the United States. He'd never stopped working long enough to court a woman and marry, although my mother tried vainly to arrange that for him a few times.

The last time I saw John Catsulis was at my mother's funeral. He must have been around ninety then, the hair at his temples grown white, his strong, stocky body more stooped than I remembered. He stood beside my mother's coffin with tears on his cheeks. When we exchanged a few words, he gave me his address and asked me to come and see him, but I never did. After several more years had passed I assumed he must have died.

Then the phone call came from Helen Papadikes Grenus telling me of her godfather's death. He'd had a stroke in 1984 and had been confined in the hospital from then until his death. Until the stroke, at the age of ninety-six, he'd still been working in the restaurant. She sent me his obituary and in her letter wrote, "Feel at ease he had the best of care at the VA hospital. The nurses loved him and the chaplain, George Phillipas, and our priest, Father John Sardis, saw him regularly."

Like opening a musty, forgotten book, the pages fluttered. I remembered how warmly he greeted my mother and me and how I relished those berried mounds of fresh pie.

He had been, I suppose, what one might call an ordinary man, his life varying only in the degree of labor from those daily endeavors made by thousands of Greeks operating restaurants in this country. Yet I've written long enough to understand there isn't any such thing as an ordinary life. In what appears a commonplace and mundane existence, there can often be traced the dimensions of an epic. Just to speculate for a moment on the multitudes John Catsulis greeted and fed in more than eighty years—it must be a Homeric figure.

Reading his obituary, meager as obituaries are for ordinary men, I somehow felt one more page was needed before the book of his life is closed forever. In recognizing him, recall as well the fervor of his dream, which couldn't glow in the same way for me because I was born here and never experienced what he endured.

John Catsulis, born Katsoulakis in Crete in 1888, died in Chicago in 1987. All his life he labored in restaurants in the heart of that country he called, like a song or poem, Am-me-ri-ca.

Snared by a Decent Impulse at Christmas

THE MAN was walking along the shoulder of busy Algonquin Road carrying a large suitcase that he kept switching from arm to arm. From time to time he'd look back and signal with his thumb, a futile gesture since the cars never even slowed.

Having lived long enough to understand the world was a vale of struggle and heartbreak, my first impulse was to flee into my apartment. I committed the mistake of looking back for a glimpse of him before unlocking my outer door. He was crouched beside his suitcase in a posture I took to be somewhere between resignation and exhaustion.

We were fifteen miles northwest of O'Hare, and I thought perhaps his car had broken down. If he were trying to reach the Sheraton about a half-mile away, helping him would only take me a few minutes.

When I reached him I asked where he was going. He was short, with a strong, wiry build and a sun-weathered face that concealed his age within the fifties or sixties. He was neatly dressed in a worn gray suit that was frayed at the cuffs. He wore a plaid shirt and red knit tie and a shapeless felt fedora. Despite the coldness of the December day, he wasn't wearing an overcoat.

"I'm heading into downtown Chicago," he said. When I asked him how he planned to get there, he smiled a pleasant wrinkling of his brown cheeks. The smile reflected in his eyes.

"Hitchhike," he said.

"That's twenty-five miles!" I said. "Lugging that suitcase you'll have trouble making a mile. No one will pick you up along here."

"I trust in the Lord," he said, and I felt gently reproved for overlooking the obvious.

"Are you staying somewhere in Chicago?"

"Just passing through," he said. "I'm going on to Norfolk, Virginia. I have a younger brother in the Navy there. We're going to spend Christmas together."

"Are you flying or taking a bus from Chicago?"

"I don't have any money left for that," he smiled again. "I used whatever I had getting here from Butte, Montana."

An aggravation and outrage assailed me. On a decent impulse I'd gone to assist a man with some minor transportation difficulty and found myself snared in a massive logistical dilemma. He must have read my expression.

"I'll make it all right, sir," he said earnestly. "The Lord will provide."

Awed at the fortitude of his faith, I recalled my father's and mother's admonitions in my childhood when I grew fearful or upset. Have faith, they'd told me many times, and the Lord will not forsake you.

"Can't you wire your brother for money?"

"I mean to surprise him and he doesn't know I'm coming. But he's away from the base for another week until December 18." He paused. "We haven't seen each other in four years."

The cars whizzing by us made it hazardous to prolong the encounter. His problem was of a magnitude that, while any effort to help would be minuscule, I couldn't simply walk away even if he were only going to Norfolk and not to Bethlehem.

"There's a Northwestern station a few miles from here," I said. "I'll drive you there and you can catch a train into Chicago. I'll give you the money for the fare."

"Thank you kindly," he said. His thank-you was courteous and restrained, as though he had expected me to offer him some assistance.

The bulk of the suitcase as I hoisted it into the trunk of my car gave me the ominous thought that it contained stolen bullion. Even worse, the dismembered body of some unfaithful sweetheart. He climbed into the front seat beside me.

"My name's Jerry Stine," he said. I told him my name and we shook hands. I tried to discern some slackness of character in his grip.

"What business are you in?" I asked.

"I've done lots of things," he said. "Mostly farming and blacksmithing. My folks who are both dead now were farmers. So was my grandfather. What about you?"

"I'm a writer."

For the first time his face glowed with animation.

"You write stories?" he asked. I nodded.

"That's really exciting! I've always loved stories! I've never written any myself but my grandpa would tell me stories of wagon trains and Indian raids." He paused. "A writer," he said, shaking his head as if marveling at his good fortune, not in being picked up but at having been picked up by a writer. Against my will I was drawn to him.

At the railroad station I dragged his suitcase out of the trunk and he took it and carried it up the stairs. We checked the schedules and found that the next eastbound train was due in forty minutes. The fare was $3.75.

I relayed this information to him, thinking that if he were deceiving me I might spot a tremor. As a liar of some considerable ability myself, I hoped I might detect that elusive wraith in the demeanor of another. When I could find nothing to bolster my skepticism, I handed him a twenty-dollar bill, all I had in my wallet besides a couple of singles.

"That will leave you something for dinner," I said, "and maybe a night in a YMCA."

Life and heart had done their work and it was time for me to go.

"Thank you kindly," he said. "I hope the Lord will bless you and your family with a Merry Christmas." He settled himself on one of the benches, pulling the suitcase close to his knees.

I started from the station and, at the top of the stairs, looked back once more, the same error I'd made before the door of my apartment. The dismal station was deserted except for his lost, forlorn figure. I thought of my own family that would be gathering for Christmas, my youngest son flying to Chicago from Los Angeles, and a nephew flying from Denver. Perhaps Jerry Stine wouldn't make it to his brother, wouldn't get beyond Chicago. I walked back to the bench.

"Don't leave until I return," I said. "If you miss the next train there's another an hour later. Wait for me."

He gravely agreed, not asking why. Even if he'd asked, I hadn't any answer. As I walked to my car, I thought of all the reasons I might not help him. He was, after all, a stranger. I wasn't a wealthy man and, despite his sincere demeanor, he might not be telling me the truth. I was still evaluating these objections when I entered the travel agency office and sat down across from a pleasant-faced young woman.

I explained my dilemma, hoping she'd remind me I was displaying immense naiveté for a man of my years.

"That's wonderful!" she said. "You're showing the true spirit of Christmas!"

"How much is one-way fare to Norfolk?"

"I don't know," she gestured in apology. "I can't write bus tickets anyway. You can only get those at the terminal. I can check airline flights for you."

She checked and found the lowest fare was $280.

"Round trip?"

"One way."

I stared at her in dejection, planning to return to Jerry Stine in time to bid him farewell on the Northwestern.

"I can check Amtrak," she said eagerly. I agreed numbly. For the following twenty minutes she checked routes and tariffs.

"There's a train leaving in about three hours from

Union Station," she said. "He'll go from Chicago to Washington and change trains there for one going to Newport News. From there he'll transfer to a bus that will take him to Norfolk." She paused, and then said, "$131."

"This whole thing is crazy," I said. "I was just going up to my apartment. I was planning to have some Chinese food for dinner and then do some Christmas shopping. . . ."

She shook her head in sympathy and I fell silent. From somewhere I heard the ghostly beseechings of my parents.

The first train for Chicago had gone. Perhaps he'd fled on it, satisfied with my twenty dollars.

"What if he's gone when I get back and I have the ticket?"

"Bring it back and I'll write you a credit. I'll also make it nonrefundable. If he tries to cash it in, they'll just credit your account."

"What if he doesn't use it or turn it in?"

"You won't be able to get your money back."

I nodded and she wrote up the ticket. She gave me the Amtrak envelope with separate directions for the change of trains. As I rose to leave, she looked at me with a touch of tears in her eyes.

I drove back to the station. I climbed the stairs and saw the slight-figured man with the absurdly large suitcase on the bench where I'd left him. As I crossed to him, he rose.

"A train came," he said, "but I waited like you told me."

I gave him the ticket, carefully explaining the routing. He listened earnestly and calmly, as if I were providing exactly what he expected.

"This ticket isn't refundable," I said sternly.

"Why would I want to refund it?" he asked. "I thank you kindly for it. I'll pray for you too."

"Just drop me a note from Norfolk," I said.

He smiled then, a warm, enigmatic smile that became a laugh. For some reason I joined him and, in that final instant, I couldn't be sure whether we were laughing at the splendor of the deception or because we'd shared a unique moment of fortuitous destiny planned by someone else.

Then we parted, two men who would probably never see one another again in our lifetimes.

◢ WORLD ◣

First Visit to Greece

A CHILLED and oppressive beginning to a journey I have been waiting to make all my life. I have never been to Greece, and yet, from that myth-laden land I have drawn the emotional and spiritual sustenance for my books and stories. Now the dream is on the way to reality with certain obstructions. The charter plane is hours late in departing, the terminal at O'Hare packed with the more than 250 passengers and perhaps a thousand relatives seeing them off. Finally, at 1 a.m. we board the plane. The rows of seats, six abreast with a narrow aisle between, stretch into infinity. I have flown a great deal, been frightened a few times, but now I am terrified with a feeling there are far too many of us cramped into inadequate space. For a moment I consider turning back, taking my wife, sons, and myself off the plane. Instead I slide into the narrow, tight seat and wait apprehensively.

Impossible to imagine that the overloaded behemoth will ever take off, but it does. We are airborne waiting for the champagne flight and open bar the travel agency advertised. We are told by a stewardess there is no liquor of any kind on board. There is, however, a shortage of water.

Unscheduled stop in Bangor, Maine. Rumor crosses the plane that the pilot wants to say farewell to his mother.

Over the Atlantic in the first hours of our flight, I twist in fitful spasms, unable to sleep. All around me passengers are curled, crimped, and kinked in the paralyzing tightness of the seats. I recall a friend who had returned from Greece on a similar flight and gone directly from the airport to a hospital and into traction. I try to rest, my wife holding my hand to calm me, grateful that my sons are asleep. I have a dream in which the two colonic travel agents who handled the details of the flight are found on our plane and strangled by putting them in two seats and then pushing the seats in front of them back against their throats. I wake smiling at their choked and anguished cries.

Scheduled stop in Shannon. A bountiful oasis of duty-free cashmere sweaters, fine woolen jackets and dresses, and best of all, a bar glittering with bottles of whisky, scotch, and gin. I fight my way to a stool. Drinking, I watch the ruddy, attractive faces of the Irish girls, a slight trilling of syllables rendering their voices musical to the ear. The men are tall, lean, with curly hair. I am reminded these are James Joyce's and Sean O'Casey's people. We are to remain in Shannon forty-five minutes but are delayed again and stay three hours.

The flight resumes and, tardily, superfluously, we are served our first drinks. Two cocktails apiece in small, ready-mixed bottles. I store them in my attache case and prepare for dinner.

We are not getting dinner. Instead, somewhere between Shannon and Athens the stewardesses begin serving cake and coffee. A spell of turbulence flashes on the "Fasten Seat Belts" sign, and the serving is discontinued about a third of the way thru the plane. When they begin serving again, they have switched to apples and oranges, starting with the same passengers who had already received coffee and cake. There are howls of hunger and protest, a few passengers crying for an apple or orange as if they are starving. I think the smothering confinement and the abysmal disorder of our winged steerage has a deteriorating effect on morale.

Approaching the airport in Athens, the mood of the passengers changes. A festive excitement sweeps over us, people wandering up and down the narrow aisle, laughing and talking, ignoring the stewardess's pleas and commands to take our seats. We peer out of the windows at the lights glittering far below, our eyes searching for the lighted Parthenon. I recall the words of Pindar: "The gleaming, and the violet crowned, and the sung in story; the bulwark of Hellas, famous Athens, city divine!" We land at 2 a.m. Athens time.

On the ground, motor buses take us from the airplane to the terminal. Another mob scene as we try to assemble our luggage. Afterwards, weary and irritated passengers try to find taxis. The moment one appears in the square outside the airport exit, a couple of dozen people descend furiously upon it. A few of the more agile ones run alongside trying to open the door and hurl themselves in. One woman who loses a close contest vents her frustration by beating on the roof of the taxi with her umbrella. I catch a glimpse of the outraged face of the driver as he speeds by. A few people send their porters a few blocks away to bring back a taxi. Growing wearier by the moment, seeing the exhausted faces of my wife and children, I send off my porter with five dollars. He returns with a taxi ten minutes later, sitting beside the driver, the doors locked against the assaults of the crowd. When they stop before us, I hustle my family inside as he throws our luggage into the trunk, and what remains onto our laps. We drive off past the miserable faces of those still left behind.

Arrive at the Athens-Hilton at 4 a.m. Our reservations have been canceled because of the late arrival. Chalk up another score for our ubiquitous travel agents. I pledge fervently to immortalize them in a story someday. For the moment I joke, cajole, threaten, plead, until someone finds us a room, two additional cots set up for the boys. We shower, climb gratefully into our beds to sleep on Greek soil for the first time, thru nine floors of the Hilton.

Lunch the first day with an American businessman who has been in Greece for a year. He talks of the rule of the Junta as a "transitional necessity." I ask him what he feels they have accomplished. "They have reduced the bribery that was prevalent at all levels of government before," he says, "and put an end to the anarchy. Most of the people are sympathetic to them." I ask him about the continuing martial law. "It's here," he shrugs, "but you see little evidence of it in the streets. No tanks and few soldiers."

Twilight in Athens. My wife, sons, and I walk around Constitution Square, wending our way thru the throngs of people on the walks, passing thousands more sitting in the

great islands of the outdoor cafes. The night is fragrant, in-
ducing an exhilaration that sharpens impressions of everything. The men are handsome and dark-haired, talking to
one another with brisk and volatile gestures of heads and
hands. The girls are lovely, sun-bronzed, moderately mini-
skirted, barelegged, ungirdled, with barely any makeup.
They walk in a lithe half-dance, radiating a marvelous sen-
suality. The trolley buses rumble past, the taxis darting
around them like whippets circling a bear. Before the sump-
tuous Grande Bretagne and King George hotels, the elegant
doormen open taxi doors and bow out the passengers.
Above the noises of the traffic are the seething sounds of
people's voices, like the crying of thousands of birds. And
on the hill of the Acropolis, the light-garlanded columns of
the Parthenon shimmer with the radiance of a midnight
sun. I feel I have come home.

The first of our tours in Athens to the Archaeological
museum. Our guide is a rasping-voiced, dumpy-bodied,
puffy-cheeked, slit-eyed, querulous, and sardonic Greek
who radiates dignity as he speaks to us in a secular epiph-
any of Greece and Greek art.

The most impressive sight in the museum is the magnificent, viridescent bronze Poseidon, a giant sculpture of a
naked, powerful male, arms outflung, legs braced apart,
bearded head like the unyielding figurehead of a ship. Every
flowing muscle seems magnetic and alive. The cavernous
hollows in place of eyes suggest a scornful, self-inflicted
blindness that contains and understands, without seeing,
all the wonder and terror of the earth. The godlike, de-

monic form casts its spell over us all. Our guide relishes our awe for several minutes before he speaks.

"Look upon this figure well," he says, in his harsh, grating voice, "and when you return to your countries, keep it in back of your eyes. For this bronze is to sculpture what the Parthenon is to architecture and the great Greek tragedies are to drama."

We move off to inspect other artifacts of antiquity, many possessed of a startling beauty, but our glances keep returning toward the room where the stunning bronze stands. We pass, finally, out of the museum thru groups of German, Italian, and French tourists led by their guides. We are like flocks of sheep being tended by zealous shepherds, the rallying cry of our own guide as we stray or lag behind, "English-speaking people, follow me!"

First night out of Piraeus on the *Jason* bound for Crete. I stand on the forward deck just below the bridge, watching the prow of the ship leaping thru the water, the billows whirling off into the darkness on either side. A full moon bursts in a white, foaming spray across the water.

I have an eerie sense of flying swiftly toward the dark and mysterious land of my ancestors, island of the labyrinth and of the double ax, island of my father and my mother, beloved earth of Nikos Kazantzakis. It is almost as if I can hear the heartbeat of that island growing in strength and power as we draw closer, as if I can miraculously see in the distant night-clouds the peaks of the white mountains of Crete. I stand there in the dark for hours, unwilling to relinquish the exhilaration and the strange, overwhelming joy.

We dock at dawn in the harbor of Herakleion, the port appearing shabby and commonplace after the anticipation and excitement I felt the night before. Buses are lined up waiting for us on the dock. We drive thru the narrow streets of the city, signs of demolition and construction everywhere. The men on the streets appear darker, taller than the mainland Greeks I have seen so far. On a corner we pass an old white-bearded patriarch fully attired in the native vrakes, dark baggy trousers, black boots, and a beaded red and black vest. I don't know if he is an anachronism in the streets of Herakleion or whether he is there to provide atmosphere for the tourists.

On the short ride to Knossos, the earth stretches away from the road in gentle, sloping hills. Small white stone and mortar houses, often in need of paint, dot the land. Sunbrowned and barefoot children wave to us as we pass. A man walks by leading a donkey with a load of wood on its back. We pass a grove of olive trees that resembles a horde of twisted and withered old crones, limbs bent toward the earth in supplication or up to the sky in lament.

We walk thru the rooms of the palace at Knossos, the remnants of the great Minoan civilization that shone brilliantly for almost five hundred years, from about 2000 to 1500 B.C. The art, the design, the exquisite frescoes depicting the slim, graceful youths leaping over the heads of bulls, all manifest a remarkable culture which once existed. Then fire and pillage came at the hands of invaders whose identity remains undisclosed to this day. All that is left of the once-mighty civilization are the restorations here and the fragments in museums. Where kings and courtiers once walked, now, thousands of years later, tourists wander, feeling the wind whistling eerily around the columns and over the stones.

Even our guide seems to have assimilated the somberness of the surroundings. She is a little Cretan girl named Rena, precise in her use of English, time and ages removed from the gilded and bejeweled figures of the courtesans and queens in the frescoes and paintings. In a faded, plain blue smock, her dark eyes large and serious within the shell frame of her glasses, her voice is grave as she speaks of the vanished civilization. Now and then she slips off one shoe; her small, bare foot, slim-boned and brown from the sun, toes pale as tiny fluted seashells, rubs the ankle of her other leg. She slips her foot back into the shoe and leads us thru the throne room, the queen's bath, the House of Frescoes, with an unmistakable authority and pride, as if these fragments of the colossus belong to her alone now.

Back in Herakleion with an hour remaining before our ship is to depart, I hail a cab and ask the driver how long it will take to drive to the grave of Nikos Kazantzakis and back to the harbor. He assures me we can do it in plenty of time. We drive thru the streets of Herakleion to park at the base of the stone steps leading up to the bastion of the old Venetian fortress wall where the greatest of the modern Greeks lies buried. We walk up the steps and when we reach the top, I see the grave, solitary and stark in the afternoon sun. It lies in the center of the bastion, four great stones symbolizing the regions of Crete, at their heads a tall, simple wooden cross. It might have been the cross of some early Christian martyr, reminiscent of a time when the wellsprings of faith were still vital and nourishing. On the stone below the cross are carved the words Kazantzakis had chosen for his epitaph: "I do not fear anything. I do not hope for anything. I am free."

The roofs of the city stretch out in tiers below. The scents of the sea bring a piquant and pleasant sharpness to the air. In the distance a range of majestic mountains thrust their plumed peaks into the sky. It is the kind of surroundings he would have chosen, to be buried within the embrace of the primal elements, overlooking his beloved Crete.

I think of the beginning of his *Report to Greco,* the autobiography written near the end of his life: "I collect my tools: sight, smell, touch, taste, hearing, intellect. Night has fallen, the day's work is done. I return like a mole to my home, the ground. Not because I am tired and cannot work. I am not tired. But the sun has set."

Standing before the grave with the Cretan taxi driver, I am not sure whether I begin to cry because I see him cry, or whether he cries when I begin to cry, but for whatever reasons were personal to us, we cry together. By that act of common devotion we form a bond, the two of us suddenly forged as close as if we are brothers or have been friends for years.

We start down the steps of the fortress. He pauses for a moment and when I stop, he stares intently into my face.

"You are a writer and you love Kazantzakis," he says. "Go back to America and write the truth of what is happening here."

"What is the truth?" I ask him.

"The truth is they have done some good things to help the people," he says. For a moment he stands silent looking over the rooftops of the city. "But as long as we are not free to speak what we think, we are not really alive." He points back up the steps toward the grave. "He would have understood."

Santorini . . . a strange, fierce island of gaunt, sheer cliffs, an island born when a volcano rose from the sea in prehistoric times. We are anchored in the harbor, waiting for the launches to carry us thru the choppy waters to shore, staring up at a sheer mountain of rock, vestiges of gray lava, and white stone. A narrow, precipitous path zigzags its way up the rock and on top a cluster of white houses seem to hang on the peaks. In 1956 a savage earthquake, the most recent of a series of eruptions, drove thousands of the inhabitants away. But almost sixteen thousand men, women, and children stubbornly remain.

We climb out of the launches and wait to mount the donkeys and mules for the perilous climb to the top. The animals are believed by the islanders to contain the souls of the dead, and the task of carrying us up the steep steps is their purgatory.

Perched in the saddles we laugh and giggle like children suspended between terror and delight. A muleteer, most often a man but sometimes a woman, starts the animals up the steps with shouts and lashes across the flanks. We begin the ascent, meeting tourist-laden animals led by their drivers coming down. We laugh and greet one another, but the muleteers do not laugh. Somber and unsmiling, they are dark, sun-blackened figures that might have been carved from the molten rock of the volcano itself. The men wear caps, shirts with long sleeves. The women with their heads cowled and long black skirts. Their wrists and hands spring from the sleeves of their clothing like husks and roots from the earth. Forty minutes of steep ascent each time they go up, almost the same amount of time coming down, an average of twenty grueling trips a day. I am suddenly, oppressively aware how much they resemble the weary beasts that carry us. I feel a rampant compassion for them, for their own purgatory. I wonder why they remain, reconciled to such unending labor, on an island which might erupt again at any time.

We dismount at the top in the village of Thira, a community of white-washed houses, shops, and churches. There is a shrill, curious moaning in the air. After a moment I realize it is the wind, but a wind unlike any I have ever heard before. I walk out of the protection of the buildings and feel the wind pull and tug wildly at my face and clothing. I brace myself and move to the edge of a parapet. As I look over the stone ledge I have the feeling of standing at some vantage point above the earth, looking at a world of rampant beauty.

The white-cubed houses, brilliant red geraniums in their windows, and the churches with small cupolas hang on the sheer side of the cliffs. Above them a peacock-blue sky trails plumes of mist to the sea, shimmering a deep purple, in the late afternoon. On the horizon gleam the shadowed, almost black, fragments of other islets.

I understand, suddenly, that the people of Santorin

exist in a boundary-world of war between gods and mortals. They are lashed by thunder and fire, the sun withers and blackens their flesh, like Sisyphus they push stones endlessly up and down the mountain. Still they cling grimly and obstinately to the sheer, tortuous rock, possessed by the island's stunning primal beauty, bound by a fierce pride in their ability to survive. They must know that some day, inevitably, the island will be swallowed once more by its mother, the sea. Until then they struggle, enduring what the errant and capricious gods seek to make unendurable.

We sail from the Sea of Marmara into the straits of the Bosporus, the waterway separating Europe from Asia. Enthroned on the European side, on seven hills lying close to the dark, swift-moving water, is the city of Istanbul. For Greeks thruout the world it remains and will always remain Constantinople, the holy city of Justinian and Constantine I.

There are modern buildings along the shore, elegant hotels, alongside old fortresses with turreted walls, the domes of countless mosques broken by the spears of minarets. From the vantage point of our ship, over the expanse of water, there is a strange beauty to the skyline. One is reminded of Hollywood films made years ago with the stories set in exotic Baghdad and Samarkand.

When we dock and disembark, first passing the somber inspection of Turkish officials, we emerge from the port into the city. Our tour buses move slowly and burdensomely into streets teeming with autos, bicycles, mules, carts, wagons, and the "hamali," the men with great tiers of boxes strapped on their backs, their bodies bent almost double under the load. As the traffic crawls in the pace of myriad snails, the hamali scurry thru the maze, adroitly and miraculously, considering their staggering loads, dodging bumpers, wheels, and hooves. We seem instantly to have been hurled into the past.

Standing under the soaring dome of the great Hagia Sophia cathedral, the masterpiece of Byzantine architecture built by the Emperor Justinian in 532–537, a feeling of sadness sweeps over me. One can imagine the fiery, encrimsoned brilliance of the cathedral as it must have been during the days of the Byzantine emperors. Now it seems enveloped and cinctured by neglect, a gray dreariness, a heavy, leaden silence. When Constantinople fell to Sultan Mohammed II in 1453, the church was converted into a mosque, the interior mosaics obscured under coatings of plaster and painted ornaments. In 1935, Kemal Ataturk designated it a museum.

So, in 1969, like a desolate and deserted castle, it whispers the glory of a once-great past. Wherever one stands and looks up, the huge disks with crescents obliterate any sign of the cross.

Outside the cathedral on our way back to the buses, the vendors and beggars besiege us, selling slides, postcards, souvenirs of the great tomb.

Late that afternoon, a group of the Greek-Americans traveling on our ship, about 35 men, women, and children, are granted an audience with His Holiness, Patriarch Athenagoras I, at 81 years of age the spiritual leader of more than 160 million members of Eastern Orthodox Christianity.

A bus carries us to the Phanar quarter, once a fashionable Greek neighborhood but now a Turkish slum. The Patriarchion, consisting of a three-story main building, a service building, and a small church, is set within a walled enclosure. Inside the courtyard there are gardens of flowers in warm and variable hues, a vivid profusion of reds and pinks, purples and yellows.

We are led up the steps into the main building, thru silent, bare, and shadowed corridors, to a corner office that, for a moment, I imagine belongs to a secretary. Then, over the heads of the people in front of me I see the black-robed, black-capped, and towering figure of the patriarch rise to greet us. One by one we enter the austere and sparsely furnished office, kissing his hand, receiving his blessing and embrace. The young priest and another aide keep bringing in chairs until we are all finally seated in a semicircle around his desk, the children in the chairs closest to the patriarch. When he sits down, an uneasy suspense holds us in silence. One of the children coughs, several men clear their throats nervously, a woman drops her purse and her husband glares at her.

Then, the majestic old man with the flowing, gray beard, white bushy eyebrows, bright and discerning eyes smiles, a quick quivering of the strands of beard around his mouth. And with the warm, encompassing smile, the laughter in his eyes, we visibly relax.

"Tell me about America," he says, and his voice is soft and resonant. We look at one another, uncertain where to begin or what to tell him, and he, seeking to put us further at our ease, begins quietly to talk of watching American television for hours every day. For a moment we are puzzled, until, a prankish glitter in his eyes, he informs us the television set is in his head, consisting of all the memories of American people and places he had seen during his sojourn in the United States from 1930 to 1948. Very rapidly he charms and possesses us all. The children smile at him, and we adults nod at one another in unrestrained approval.

"Tell me about America," he says again.

A few members of our group now speak up, telling him of the building of a new church, the success of a fund-raising drive for the Greek orphanage, victory for some young Greeks in a sports tournament. He listens intently, nodding with satisfaction. When we fall silent again, waiting for him to speak, he talks with genuine affection of the United States, of the basis of our existence in this country being spiritual, humanistic, and philanthropic. He speaks with fervor and conviction. I cannot help thinking for a moment of the murders of John and Robert Kennedy and the Rev. Martin Luther King Jr., of the war in Viet Nam, of the many manifestations in our society of sickness and violence.

He talks of the friendship existing between the Turks and Greeks still remaining in Istanbul, points proudly to the picture of Kemal Ataturk on his office wall. Someone asks him if the Greeks of Istanbul are in any danger in the continuing Turkish resentment over Cyprus, whether some flareup or worsening of the crisis might not produce, as it has in the past, a rampage of violence and destruction. At mention of Archbishop Makarios of Cyprus, he shakes his head somberly. "I regret to say that Makarios does not want union with Greece. No, not at all." But, in spite of this constant source of friction in the relationship between Greeks and Turks, he firmly reassures us of his conviction that his flock and he are perfectly safe in Istanbul. When someone else asks him how many Greeks remain in Istanbul, he answers slowly, "We are few and uncounted." And somehow his caution reveals and expresses more than all his words of reassurance.

Having often been visited by Greek-Americans before, knowing their propensity for pictures, he suggests we go outside into the garden to take pictures while there is still daylight. He gathers a group of the children in the circle of his arms, close to the folds of his cassock, and we follow him down the corridors and outside into the garden. For almost an hour in the waning afternoon sun, within the fragrance of the garden, the children and their parents take turns clustering around his tall, lean, and stately figure, while others snap endless shutters.

When we have taken our fill of pictures, he bids us good-by with almost a kind of sadness. One by one we kiss his hand and are warmed by his embrace. Afterward we straggle toward the gate, to the bus waiting for us outside. He walks up the steps to the doorway of the building and turns. He waves to us slowly and we wave back, and I marvel at the way his black-robed figure radiates even over the distance that separates us, a strange, piercing beauty of soul, a profusion of love.

That is our last sight of Patriarch Athenagoras, his figure standing in the doorway above the blooming flowers of the garden, while from beyond the walls that circle the Patriarchion, the harsh, astringent sounds of Istanbul carry like the ominous rumble of an advancing army.

On one of our final evenings in Athens before leaving Greece for home, my wife and I are guests of the gracious undersecretary to the prime minister, at the Dionysus restaurant, a dinner attended by about fifty people. We sit at a long table on the roof garden of the restaurant. Across from us, on the peak of the Acropolis, the illuminated Parthenon glows against the starry, night sky. The vision is one of an exhilarating and ageless beauty that flows into the eyes and into the heart.

I sit thinking of the weeks we have spent traveling across Greece from Salonika to the mountains of Crete, from Santorini to Istanbul, the myriad faces and voices of people in the villages and in the towns. The reality for me was even greater than the expectation and I am sorry that within a few days we will be leaving. And I wonder, too, what the months to come hold for the small, hallowed country that has suffered so much for so many centuries of war, famine, and poverty.

I am returned from my thoughts to the reality of men's voices speaking, words reaffirming the dedication of the new government, its aspirations and its divine mission. The men who speak seem evidently sincere in believing that what is being done is for the welfare of Greece and the Greek people. Yet I cannot help feeling their words have a spectral transience under the magnificence of the Parthenon. The temple has a resonance that extinguishes mere words, a resonance that is both an apotheosis and a warning. Tyrants and demagogs, Romans and Visigoths, Venetians and Turks, all have passed beneath its columns and all are gone. The Parthenon remains. The lesson for those who understand history is that whoever aspires to guide the destiny of the country the temple protects, must challenge the implacable scale of more than two thousand years.

For even colonels die. Their words and deeds pass away. The Parthenon remains. Yet, even if the columns of the temple were razed and leveled, men and women for ages to come would still journey to the place where the temple stood to reflect on how stones and ruins can still guard and nourish a tradition that will forever remain the strength and greatness of Hellas.

Letters from Israel

June 13, 1970

DEAREST FAMILY:

Altho I have been in Israel for three days now, I have not stopped moving long enough to begin a coherent letter. The impressions of the last few days are so full and diverse, it is difficult to know where to begin.

On the night of my arrival at Lod Airport in Tel Aviv, tall and courtly Amnon Gil-Ad of the ministry of tourism met me and we drove thru the cool and fragrant night to Jerusalem. Along the highway, lights, gleaming in the windows of houses, resembled the landscape from highways we drive at night in America.

Before checking into the King David Hotel where I would be staying, I asked Amnon to take me to the Western or Wailing Wall. We parked outside the guard's checkpoint and saw the wall brightly lit by floodlights. As we started thru the gate, a platoon of young Israeli soldiers who had been praying at the wall straggled back to their guns stacked in the courtyard. The rattle of arms and the banter of their voices faded as they boarded their trucks and departed. The wall was left silent except for two old Orthodox

Jews in caftans with sidecurls dangling from beneath their wide black hats. One rested his head motionless against the wall while the other swayed and chanted softly in prayer.

I walked to the wall and stood for a moment before it. The stones at the base were great boulders, growing smaller as the tiers ascended, the parapet seeming to disappear into the darkness of the star-flecked sky. Within the cracks between the stones were stuffed thousands and thousands of tightly folded pieces of paper containing prayers.

At Delphi, in Greece, where I had been a few days earlier, I had walked in a timeless world among majestic mountains, the sea misted and shimmering in the distance. Feeling the resonances of my heritage, I had accepted the presence of ghosts and spirits among the white sculptured ruins of altars and temples.

I had not anticipated that I would feel such a resonance in Israel. After all, it is not my country either by blood or by birth. But I have experienced an intense and curious affinity with people and places here the last few days, a synonymity with the sustaining power of their tradition that began with the first night in Jerusalem before the great Wailing Wall. I had a kind of indefinable recognition that I shared the experience of the wall. I bent then and kissed the ancient stone. When we left the courtyard, the old Orthodox Jew still chanted his prayers, his voice whirling softly into the night.

Early the following morning, the guide that the ministry had assigned to me picked me up at the hotel. His name is Eli Spector, and he is a grizzled, strong and very courteous Sabra, a native-born Israeli. Indeed, he is very much like the cactus from which the word Sabra is derived. His hair is frizzled, the flesh of his face creased and engraved with myriad lines. His eyes seem to have formed an extra layer of protective appendage against the sun, and when he smiles, only wrinkled slits are visible under his brows. But he is one of the most remarkable men I have ever met, assured and gentle in his strength, with a soul full of passion and love for Israel. I was reminded again with Eli of the ways in which men are irrevocably bound to the fragments of earth they feel contain their roots.

The first day we spent driving around Jerusalem. The Knesset, the modern parliament building, and the Shrine of the Book in the Israel Museum, which contains the Dead Sea Scrolls, are sharply contrasted with the old houses of Jerusalem stone, arched windows, ironwork grilles and metal doors. Except for the skeletons of new apartment buildings rising on the perimeters of the city, one imagines the physical setting almost unchanged from biblical times.

This sense of the immediacy of the past is given sharper impetus when one enters the walled Old City. We walked the narrow, winding streets full of smells, cries, and teeming crowds, haggling, bargaining with the merchants of the hundreds of shops and stalls. They sell curios, religious mementoes, lemonade, pitta, vegetables, fruit, and the desiccated chickens, plucked and forlorn, that hang from the rows of hooks. In the cafés, Arabs sit somberly smoking the nargilah, the long-stemmed water pipes. Thru the streets past them throng old Orthodox Jews in their stockinged legs and black fur hats, their sons following at their heels, looking like miniature versions of their fathers. There are bearded Greek Orthodox monks, dark-skinned Yemenites, Druze soldiers, Arab women with their faces veiled and their eyes downcast. (I am afraid none of them resemble Yvonne DeCarlo.) But the centuries seem wiped away, and we could well be in the time when Jesus walked these same streets along the Stations of the Cross, the route He walked on the way to His crucifixion.

Afterwards, from the peak of the Mount of Olives, we looked down upon the stunning panorama of the city dominated by the golden Dome of the Rock that glistened in the sun. A small Arab child left a crowd of children gathered a few hundred feet away from us and came to offer me a small sprig of olive from the mount. Eli gave him a small Israeli coin, and the child's sharp black eyes smoked in disappointment. I gave him an American dollar, and he stared at it in shock. Then he flew back to the crowd of children.

"You are going to get it now," Eli laughed, and he motioned me quickly into the car. As we began crawling slowly and carefully forward, the mass of children gathered shrieking alongside, while Eli honked and tried to wave them away. As our path cleared, we started moving faster and the children fell behind. Only the little boy with the bright dark eyes and the beguiling smile who had given me the sprig of olive ran alongside, waving the dollar in a grateful gesture of delight.

Mount Herzl is the memorial park enclosing the tomb of Theodore Herzl, the founder of modern Zionism. The flower-garlanded park was serene in the sunlight, the grave an impressive, unadorned stone. Across the tomb from us stood an Israeli father and his son of about ten, the father speaking quietly but intensely to the boy, from time to time motioning to the tomb. I could not understand the words he spoke in Hebrew, but it was evident he was trying to communicate his allegiance and devotion to the dead hero. The child listened, yet there was that slight withdrawal about his eyes and lips that suggested he was being asked for a reverence he could not muster.

I was reminded of the father and his young son again when we entered Yad Vashem, the memorial to the 6 million Jews who died in the death camps of Hitler's Reich. We entered a rectangular building, the walls of hewn basalt boulders. The ceiling looms above a gray mosaic floor on which are inscribed the names of the twenty-one largest concentration and death camps. Belsen, Dachau, Buchenwald. . . . In the center of the floor burns an eternal light.

It is a chilling and savage experience to walk thru the exhibition, past the huge, blown-up photographs of the inmates of the camps. Behind strands of real barbed wire the haunted, emaciated and suffering faces of men, women, and children stare out at us. Their eyes reflect a timeless anguish, a terrible despair. Their faces do not accuse, nor do they hope.

I could imagine the father on Mount Herzl leading his son thru the exhibition at Yad Vashem as well. A harsh and searing experience for a child but one that might serve a purpose in reaffirming the conviction that freedom must be retained at the cost of life itself. In such a way and for that reason did the father of Nikos Kazantzakis make the child embrace and kiss the feet of Greeks hanged by the Turks, to burn upon the terrified child's soul forever the cause for which they died.

It was a relief to walk back out into the sunlight, to breathe in the fertile beauty of the earth. Yet a cold remained at the marrow of my bones for hours afterwards.

On the morning of the third day, we drove to Jericho. The landscape of the desert between Jerusalem and Jericho is unlike any section I have ever seen before, a nebulous blending of pinks and grays shimmering in the haze of heat. This is the barren wasteland where Bishop Pike left the road and wandered to his death. I could understand how merciless the sun-scorched terrain might be to a man on foot.

Jericho is not only the oldest city in the world, more than six thousand years old, but at one thousand feet below sea level it is the lowest. It is also a lush, unbelievably green oasis in the middle of the arid desert. The groves are green and fertile, and the flaming red poinciana trees dominate land and sky. All are nourished by the springs of sweet, fresh water in the ground, the spring named after Elisha, disciple of Elijah, who purified its waters.

Jericho is an Arab city, and everywhere along the streets and within the shops there is evidence of the congeniality of the thousands of Arabs living within the boundaries of Israel toward the Israelis. That is not the impression we have reading the war dispatches back home. They are friendly and banter with Eli and are formal and courteous to me. As we left the city after eating lunch, we passed beneath a minaret from whose tower a muezzin cried forth his summons for the faithful to pray.

From Jericho we drove to the edge of the Dead Sea. We changed into our swimming trunks and entered water so thick and full of minerals the surface seemed an oily and turgid crust. The water of the Dead Sea is ten times saltier than the water of the oceans, and Eli warned me about getting it into my eyes where it burns like fire. You know my penchant for salt, and just to reassure myself that nothing could be too salty, I tasted a drop of water on the tip of my finger. A shudder swept my entire body. As an old salt-user, I had found my Waterloo.

Despite Eli's promise that it is impossible for anyone to sink in the waters of the Dead Sea, I floated apprehensively, a lugubrious barge in constant danger of capsizing. Eli relaxed in obvious delight at the chance to show off, his powerful arms propelling him buoyantly thru the water while he robustly sang. Afterwards, we showered to wash the salt off our bodies and dressed and started back to Jerusalem.

Now, much later this same evening, having written you a long letter at the end of a long day, I am tired and will end. Very early in the morning Eli will pick me up and we will drive to Arad, a town newly built in the desert, so that at dawn on the following day we can climb Masada. I will write again after that experience and meanwhile I love you and miss you. Last night as I waited outside the hotel for Amnon and his wife Tamar to pick me up for dinner, I inhaled a scent similar to the scents carried by the winds of autumn back home. I felt the first sharp pangs of homesickness since leaving for Greece three weeks ago. I think it is good to travel and we should travel. But even when traveling, one must have some place to think of as home. And you are my home.

With love,

June 15, 1970

Dearest Diana, Mark, John, and Dean:

I cannot easily describe the awesome feelings I had standing on the soaring heights of the mountain fortress, Masada, in the Judean desert. One has a sense of being suspended between sky and earth, a cosmic awareness similar to that I felt on the peaks of Santorini. Both places seem to expand the boundaries of man's vision to infinity.

Masada is the site of the last stand of the Jews in their rebellion against Rome in 73 B.C. When Titus captured Jerusalem and destroyed the Temple, a group of one thousand men, women, and children fled to Masada. For three years they held out under siege by Roman armies. When the Romans finally built a huge ramp of earth up the side of the mountain and the fall of Masada was inevitable, the one thousand men, women and children in the fortress decided on a mass suicide.

There is an eerie silence across the levels and tiers of stone, the remnants of the hanging gardens, the frescoes, the throne room where Herod once walked. More than thirteen hundred feet below in the desert, the ringed campsites of the Romans are still marked. In the distance the Dead Sea seems little more than a pond.

Masada is a symbol of resistance in Israel today. The night before we climbed the mountain, several thousand young Israeli soldiers, boys and girls, climbed the peak from the serpentine path on the Dead Sea side. In a torchlight ceremony swearing them into the defense forces of the state, they pledged, "Masada shall not fall again."

And the tourists come by the busload to make the climb up the easier path, holding grimly to the handrails, pausing every few moments to renew their labored breath. Somehow, despite their pilgrimage, they all seem to look like tourists everywhere. Knock-kneed, disjointed, chip-boned, wearing a weird assortment of clothing topped by the absurd little dunce caps distributed by the tour agencies to protect their heads from the sun. But despite their appearance, they must be given points for their valor. They might have remained back at the hotel as did the woman we found crumpled like a squid in her deck chair beside the swimming pool when Eli and I returned. Eli asked her why she had not gone with the others to climb the fortress. "I'm not historical," the lady answered. "If there was a nightclub with Johnny Carson on top, I'd be the first one up. But for mountains I'm not historical."

For a moment I thought Eli might heave her into the pool, but he is too professional a guide and he simply jumped into the water himself.

By noon of that same day we were ready to leave the Nof Arad hotel. The Russian Jewish husband and wife who were the proprietors had been exceedingly gracious to me during our stay, and as we exchanged our good-bys, they asked my reactions to the mountain fortress. I told them how awed and moved I had been. And the woman, speaking only a little English, said to me sadly, "All Israel is now Masada."

As Eli and I drove away, they stood on the stoop of the hotel and waved a final farewell, a graying, aging man and woman who had spent their lifetime in quest for an existence of peace that now threatened to elude them once more.

I have forgotten to write you that all across Israel, hitchhiking is a common and popular form of transport. At every major intersection, at least a score and often many more people, usually boy and girl soldiers, waited to be picked up. We have carried at least thirty in the last few days in sets of three to fit the rear seat of our car. They are alert and handsome young people, their seminal youth and bursting good health giving them a natural beauty. Because their skin is so often bronzed by the sun, when they smile or laugh their teeth gleam like bands of ivory.

Most of them spoke some English, and when Eli told them I was a writer from America visiting Israel for the first time, they were eager for my impressions, pleased with what I had to say. When I asked for their views on America, some shrugged sheepishly and would not answer and some answered with cautious evasions. But a few boldly criticized the war in Southeast Asia, our mistreatment of our minorities. Sometimes their companions, by a look or a jab, tried to silence the outspoken ones even tho Eli and I urged them to speak frankly. I think I understood that their caution came because they didn't want to impugn their allies and friends. The spectre of the Soviet Union was very real and menacing to them. They did not display any reticence in criticizing some of the policies of their own government, they evidenced no eagerness at the prospect of war, wanted peace so they could pursue their studies and marry and raise families. But their resolve to fight to the death to retain their freedom came across to me clearly. They were not professional soldiers, simply strong and tension-tempered young people who knew their history and would never endure exile again.

All my love,

June 17, 1970

Dearest Family:

Today we drove the road from Beit Shean north to Tiberius, a road that runs parallel to the Jordan River separating Israel from Jordan. There was very little traffic on the road because of the danger of shelling from the Jordanian batteries in the mountains across the river. Above us, hidden in the cliffs, Israeli artillery waited to respond. I felt a certain uneasiness with visions of some Jordanian officer spotting our white Mercedes whipping along the road and issuing an order, "There's a presumptuous lout! Put one in his lap!" But Eli, old soldier of three wars, reflected only a moderate excitement as he hummed some martial marching song under his breath.

I think one of the loveliest sights in all Israel is to suddenly come into view of a grove of citrus trees surrounded by a perimeter of tall, verdant and regal cypresses protecting the frailer trees from the wind. Eli told me that the groves symbolized Israel itself. The fertile citrus trees were like the towns and cities, the heartland of the country, and the cypresses were like the kibbutzim along the borders that served as frontier posts long before Israel had an army, farms where people lived and worked that still served as warning outposts and as the first line of resistance against any attack.

In one of these kibbutzim under the shadow of the Jordanian mountains, a shy, barefooted little girl guided us thru the dining hall, the kitchen, and the schoolhouse. From the classrooms we descended a steep stairway into the underground bomb shelters where the children slept each night as a precaution against the shelling which might erupt at any time from the mountains across the river. The shelter had the closed, musty scents of cellars, tiers of bunks, thick metal shields for the windows, a few tables, and an assortment of toys and books.

I imagined the children sleeping when the sirens began their wail, the younger ones waking to cry, the older boys and girls trying to be brave. Locked like moles in the earth, what kind of fitful, terror-haunted sleep were they able to find?

After the shelters, we visited with several young girls in the laundry who asked me eager questions about America and laughed when I told them they were the prettiest girls I had seen in Israel. They pushed forward one of the girls, Razah, they said was a writer. She was about twenty, raven-haired and dark-eyed, with a slim, tight-fleshed face. As I might have casually asked any young man or girl back in the

United States who aspired to write, I asked her what she wrote about.

"I write of people who are afraid," she said.

Her answer chastened me because it was so obvious and fundamental a truth. Yet when I asked her again if she wanted to leave the kibbutzim, she answered, simply, once more. "No."

As we started back to our car, a group of brown, almost naked children marched in a ragged line to the swimming pool. I had seen such scenes in America many times in the parks along the lake and beaches in summer. But here they existed under an ominous shadow.

As we drove north again on the road to Tiberius, I wondered what our own reactions would be if we had to live as the parents and children of the kibbutzim. I thought of Dean, the children he played with, all the things we took for granted. I think I will never again look at children playing in the sunlight without remembering the underground shelters of the border kibbutzim.

Yet, late that night after we had returned to Tel Aviv, walking with Eli among the convivial crowds that promenaded along Dizengoff Avenue, any thought of war and the imperilment of the border seemed illusory and fanciful. Under the festive yellow and blue, red and gold glitter of the neon lights, shirt-sleeved men and lightly dressed women relished Viennese pastries and savory blintzes, sipped brandy and coffee, chattering and laughing. On the walks before the cafés, handsome young soldiers swaggered by, holding the hands of slim, lovely girls whose mini-skirts flared around their silken thighs. And in an alcove before a small crowd, an American hippie in castoff clothing played his guitar and sang in a shrill, tuneless wail while girls and young men clapped and stamped their feet in time to the rhythm.

Back in the hotel on what was my last night in Israel, I could not sleep. I sat on my balcony, overlooking the ocean and the flickering lights of the city.

I am full of the sights and sounds and smells of this resonant land. The old Bible-haunted mountains, the old men in their consecrated trappings at prayer before the wall, the black tents and grazing camels of the Bedouins in the acrid desert, Masada commanding the ghosts of Roman camps, the Sea of Galilee at twilight with the sun crimson upon the water, the hopeful faces of the young soldiers, the songs of the children, and the lovely cities, Ashkelon and Beersheba, Haifa and Hebron, Nazareth and golden Jerusalem.

In less than ten days of travel even across a small country, one cannot find answers to the grievous problems that exist: the rights of the Palestinian Arabs and the final disposition of the borders to ensure the security of Israel. But even without summary answers, one comes to understand that Israel is a symbol of man's capacity to survive, that she must endure, not only because of the suffering and the longing of centuries, but because if she does not survive, something in each of us, whether we are Jews or not, must die as well.

That is the tragedy of the tension and conflict that shadows every day and night. If her neighbors once understood that peace would bring them multiple benefits, that the deserts would bloom for them as well, then these ancient valleys and mountains might prosper and thrive.

But whether it is understood or not, Israel will survive. As she has survived centuries of exile, wandering, suffering and the holocaust of the 6 million dead. Forever looking toward that final fruition of the prophecy of Jeremiah:

> Therefore they shall come and sing in the height of Zion, and shall flow together to the goodness of the Lord, for wheat, and for wine, and for oil, and for the young of the flock and of the herd: and their soul shall be as a watered garden: and they shall not sorrow any more at all.

With all my love,
Your Wandering Greek

A Cyprus Journey

![decorative ornament] FROM THE TERRACE of my room at the Cyprus Hilton the belfries and minarets of Nicosia's churches and mosques receded across a city of white houses with red tiled roofs. In the distance a range of mountains peaked into an azure sky. Below me, waiters with trays of drinks moved among the sun worshipers basking around a huge marble swimming pool. In spite of the 1974 invasion by Turkey that partitioned the island and the city of Nicosia into Greek and Turkish zones, the tourists were coming back to Cyprus.

Although I knew that movement between the zones was forbidden, I put in a call to Husrev Suleyman of the Turkish Cypriot Information Office, explaining my wish to do a story on Cyprus and asking permission to visit the Turkish zone.

"Come on over now," he said as casually as if he were inviting me down the block for a beer.

"Do I just walk over?"

"Take a taxi to the checkpoint at the Ledra Palace," he said. "Cross over from there."

The Greek-Cypriot checkpoint at the Ledra Palace was

staffed by several policemen and soldiers. I approached one of them and showed him my passport and the letter on my assignment.

"You have a press card?"

"No. I'm a novelist. This is a special assignment."

"You have a Greek name."

"I am Greek-American."

"If you are Greek, why do you want to go over there?"

I gestured at the letter in his hands. He shrugged and took down my name and passport number.

"Are you returning tonight?"

"Yes."

"Are you sure?" His mocking tone suggested there were calamities and dangers in the Turkish zone my poor mind could not fathom.

Beyond the Greek checkpoint, a rubble of demolished buildings reminded me of urban renewal wreckage back home. Only the ugly tangle of barbed wire marked the area as a former battle zone. At the United Nations checkpoint I handed my passport and letter to a young sentry who wore the UN sleeve emblem on his uniform. "I am a journalist . . . a writer," I said.

He smiled obligingly and shook his head, conveying he could not speak English. He motioned me to sit down on a bench and walked into an adjoining shed. I could see him talking on the phone. Twenty minutes later a jeep drove up. An officer emerged and saluted me snappily.

"You are a journalist?"

"Yes."

He examined my passport. "You are Greek?"

"I am an American. I was born in St. Louis, Missouri, and raised in Chicago. My parents were Greek."

I waited uneasily while he made another phone call, speaking even more rapidly in French. When he returned, he handed me back my passport and letter with another salute. "You are free to proceed," he said. "We are sorry for the delay."

"Do they know I'm coming now?" I pointed anxiously to the Turkish checkpoint ahead.

"We don't have anything to do with them," the officer said pleasantly.

I walked on and after a couple of hundred yards approached what I recognized from the war movies as a machine gun pointing at me across a rampart of sandbags. I waved the passport and letter feebly, one in each upraised hand, like symbols of truce. The young, dark-complexioned soldier stared at me for a moment and then, looking slightly bored with my theatrics, motioned me on.

I had arrived in Cyprus, the most easterly of the Mediterranean islands, and forty miles from the Turkish mainland, just the previous day on my first visit to the island. My parents had been born on another Greek island, Crete, where, as young people, they had lived under the foreign occupation of the Ottoman Turks. As a child I listened to their chronicles about the sorrows of bondage, an agony that had driven the Cretans through two centuries of recurrent revolt, until their liberation and union with Greece in 1913. To me, as to other Greeks around the world, the kindling of a similar struggle in Cyprus in the years before World War I was the continuation of a heroic drama that began with the Greek War of Independence of 1821–1830, when, after four hundred years of bondage, the small nation won its freedom from the Turks. With the ravages of slavery so recent a part of their history, freedom to a Greek was a sacred quest.

"What first truly stirred my soul was not fear or pain, nor was it pleasure or games; it was the yearning for freedom," wrote Nikos Kazantzakis, who grew up in the enslaved Crete of my parents' time. The words of that great writer haunted every Greek soul.

To the Greek-Cypriot, the island, legendary birthplace of the goddess Aphrodite, is as Greek as the motherland itself and has been since Mycenaean times. But the Turks base their historical claims on having conquered the island in 1571. In 1878 they leased it to England (which annexed it during World War I).

In the Greek-Cypriot agitation for freedom from Britain and union with Greece following World War II, the Turkish-Cypriot minority felt themselves threatened. The independent republic founded in 1959 under Archbishop Makarios was made acceptable to the Turkish-Cypriots only by the veto powers conceded to them by its new constitution. President Makarios's attempt in 1963 to revise that constitution and the succeeding ten years of sporadic, often savage, fighting and fragile periods of truce, policed by a small United Nations peacekeeping force, were regarded by Turkish-Cypriots as a struggle for their own survival.

The 1974 invasion displaced some 200,000 Greek-Cypriots, three-fifths of their total population, driving them in waves to the southern half of the island. But Turkey claimed it had been forced to act to protect the 116,000 Turkish-Cypriots by a coup in Nicosia the previous month. The coup, coupled with an attempt to assassinate Archbishop Makarios, was plotted by the fascist colonels' junta then in power in Athens. Turkey's response was to invade the island. The threat of war between Greece and Turkey over Cyprus caused the collapse of the colonels and brought a democratic, civilian government back to Greece. President Makarios returned from exile to head the Greek-Cypriot government again, but the island remained partitioned. In the three years that had passed since the invasion, hopes for accommodation and territorial adjustments would appear in the world press, but each time the attempts would deadlock and fail.

In the sanctuary of my Midwestern home, as I read the stories of the suffering refugees from Cyprus, read the denunciations and accusations of Greek and Turkish leaders, I knew I had to visit the island myself, see the faces and hear the voices of its Turkish-Cypriots and its Greek-Cypriots. Only in that way might I come to understand whether they could live together in peace if the Turks withdrew. As I made plans for my journey, I also understood I would have to come to grips with something ancient, not easily altered, in my own heart.

The Public Information Office in the Turkish sector of Nicosia was austerely furnished. Waiting, I studied the photographs on the walls and recognized the hero of modern Turkey, Mustafa Kemal Ataturk.

Husrev Suleyman came into the room, a man in his middle thirties, as dark-haired and olive-skinned as any Greek. We shook hands and a porter brought us coffee.

For the next forty-five minutes Suleyman spoke vigorously of Greek deception, connivance, and intrigue. He scoffed at my suggestion that the Greek-Cypriots had renounced union with Greece.

"We have been hearing that lie for years. But we have recorded speeches of Archbishop Makarios and his followers stating that Cyprus has always been Greek and must someday join Greece."

I asked about the 200,000 Greek refugees. He showed me a Turkish information bulletin placing the number at 56,000.

"Even if that figure is too low, 90,000 would be closer to accurate. But 200,000? Ridiculous. Greek propaganda."

He was silent for a minute. "When our villages were attacked and burned in 1963 and 1964," he said, "25,000 of our people became refugees. They lived wretchedly as refugees for eleven years. Where was the world's concern for Cyprus suffering then?"

I asked, finally, if we could make a trip through the Turkish-Cypriot zone.

"Do you want to go now? We can go right now."

"Monday or Tuesday would be better."

"Come here at ten o'clock on Tuesday. I will take you anywhere you wish to go, north, east, or west." He shrugged. "Of course, you understand, I cannot take you south."

"Perhaps I can take you south," I smiled.

Suleyman laughed amiably at my whimsical invitation.

I had been escorted to the Information Office from the Turkish checkpoint by Hassan, a Turkish-Cypriot who had learned English at the American school in Nicosia. He had sat in on the meeting, and now escorted me back.

"America is like a father with two children," Hassan said gently. "Greece is one child and Turkey is the other child. Sometimes the father seems to favor one and sometimes the other, but both children are loved and both should understand that the father is trying to be fair."

He spoke with sympathy, as though in deference to my feelings. We shook hands warmly, and I walked back to the Greek-Cypriot zone.

At the hotel that evening I was picked up by Maria Hadjipavlou, a young Greek-Cypriot writer in the Greek Public Information Office. She was a slender, comely girl with large, compassionate eyes. Much of her work involved the refugees, and as we drove to visit the first of the camps she told me what had happened after the invasion.

When the first thousands of refugees swarmed into the south, some crowded in with relatives and friends. Others were taken in by strangers, sleeping on the floors in basements and attics. Tens of thousands camped under trees, in parks or vacant lots, building shantytowns of sacks, boxes, and crates. Toilets were holes dug into the ground, plugged up when they were full. Great quantities of soup and beans had to be prepared and distributed to avoid starvation.

As tents were shipped into the island, tent cities sprang

up. But they were little protection against the dampness and cold of winter. The refugees suffered from pneumonia, dysentery, and an epidemic of scarlet fever that struck the children.

By the beginning of the third year, refugees were moving into thousands of tract houses built by large aid grants from the UN and the United States. The conditions of those remaining in tents and shanties, while improved from the beginning, were still, Maria told me, wretched by any human standard.

II

We drove into the refugee camp along a rutted roadway, between two rows of tents. Twilight darkened the pyramids of canvas, some of them lit by the glow of candles and lanterns. A fragrance of spring fruit scented the air. There were people sitting on chairs and benches under the trees, staring at us as we passed. When we stepped out of the car, some of them recognized Maria and came to greet us.

"*Kalos orisate* . . . welcome . . . welcome . . ." Two women kissed and hugged Maria and offered their hospitality.

We entered a tent belonging to an old farmer and his wife from a village in the district of Kyrenia. He was short, with thick white hair and ruddy cheeks that made him appear a diminutive Santa Claus. His wife was a stocky younger woman, with an unnatural pallor in her cheeks that contrasted with her brown, strong hands.

"How are things going, Grandfather?" Maria asked.

He shrugged. "They could be better, they could be worse."

A votive candle threw a wavering light on the icons of the saints, with their brooding visages. Beside them was a photograph of the robed Archbishop Makarios, Ethnarch of Cyprus. (He had suffered a heart attack but was, at that time, still alive.) The tent's meager furnishings were neatly placed, with laces and fringed cloths spread over them in an effort at adornment.

"Have you heard when they will move you into a house?" Maria asked.

"Sometimes they tell us one month, sometimes three months," the woman said. "Most of the families with children in this camp have already moved, or are getting ready to move. That is the fair way, and the old man and I will wait our turn."

"If we just had a little more allowance each month," the farmer said. "The coupons they give us stay the same, but the price of food goes up." He motioned toward his wife. "She needs medicine too."

"She is diabetic and needs insulin," Maria said to me. She made a notation in her notebook.

"What are you standing around for, woman?" the farmer asked his wife gruffly. "Give our guests some coffee or juice."

I thanked them, saying I didn't care for anything, but they joined in heated protest, insisting that we have a cup of coffee, or fruit juice, or a sugared *loukoum*. I smiled sheepishly at Maria, admitting my naiveté in thinking that I could enter any Greek dwelling, even a refugee tent, without accepting that *filotimo* toward strangers, the hospitality that Greeks everywhere venerate almost as a religion.

A second tent, furnished like the first, was occupied by a shepherd and his wife who had lost their nineteen-year-old son in the 1974 invasion. The boy had resisted the Turkish soldiers and had been shot to death.

Resignation haunted their faces and shadowed their words. When Maria asked when they would be moved into one of the houses being built for the refugees, the shepherd said quietly they could share whatever became available, since they no longer need the room they had required when their son was alive.

A larger tent, connected to a shed covered by metal siding. Here the atmosphere was less somber because a child had only recently been born. The adoring glances of the handsome young mother and the sturdy grandmother never strayed far from the ebullient baby that kicked up its feet on the bed. The father and grandfather were away, having been fortunate enough to find work in Nicosia.

"We are not afraid of the future," the grandmother said. "We must be patient, grateful for God's blessings and the protection of his Beatitude, our revered Archbishop Makarios." She raised the baby lovingly from the bed. "And my grandson will see our land again. In my heart I know that to be true."

Another tent, and a taciturn man who regarded me with constrained hostility as a representative of the great power that he felt had allowed the Turks to retain the areas their armies had seized.

"Tell your President Carter I don't want his wealth," the man said as we were leaving. "I want his help only to regain my house, my patch of land, and the graveyard where my dead are buried."

We were walking back to our car when a young woman paused to speak to Maria. Even in the gathering darkness I could see she was a lovely girl, with almond eyes, and a face that recalled the melancholy beauty of the actress Irene Papas.

"She and her young man, also a refugee, will be married soon," Maria said, after the girl walked on. "They have jobs in the city and are saving money to rent and furnish a little apartment. In that way they will not have to begin life in the camp."

"There is a sorrow about her," I said. "As though she were a character in an old tragedy."

We got into the car and closed the door. "She was raped by the Turkish soldiers who took her village," Maria said. "She became pregnant, and the doctors aborted the embryo."

Back in my comfortable hotel room, I found it hard to fall asleep that night. The faces and voices of the men and women in the camp kept returning to me.

"When I go back to my land . . ."

"In my home were the possessions my mother had left me . . ."

"You could see the sea from our terrace . . ."

"I made bread in our oven on that feast day . . ."

"When we watered the apricot trees in the twilight, such a smell of sweetness rose from that fruit . . ."

The last thing I remembered before falling asleep was a strip of moonlight glistening between the drapes.

An overcast day. Clouds like gray bunting trailed over the rooftops of Nicosia. The pool area below me was deserted, the cushions stripped from the chaise lounges. A few birds skimmed over the tranquil water.

Maria picked me up early. We drove to one of the new housing settlements, a huge tract of stucco and concrete blocks, hundreds of buildings completed and hundreds still under construction. Tiny plots of flowers in circles of white-washed stone and sprigs of basil and marjoram in tin cans on the windowsills softened the depressing and monotonous surroundings.

Hearing of a woman whose husband was among those still missing, we knocked on her door. She was in her fifties, tall, strong-bodied with wrinkled temples and cheeks. She was dressed in black, and her black hair, streaked with gray, was tied back in a severe bun. Looking as if she were a visitor herself in her sparsely furnished and antiseptic rooms, she invited us to sit down. Seated across from us, she spoke in a low and mournful voice of the day the Turkish soldiers had come to her village.

When the villagers first saw the planes overhead and heard the thunder of the guns, they were confused and then afraid. Her daughter was sent away with other village girls to be hidden but she remained with her husband who would not leave their house and land. Many of the neighbors locked themselves in their houses, as though the Turks were a storm that would pass over them.

Soon afterwards the Turkish soldiers entered the village and battered down the doors. They dragged people out, cursing the women and kicking and beating some of the men. The village priest suffered the most abuse, his cassock torn off, his beard and hair pulled until he shrieked and bled. Finally, the rings pulled off their fingers, separated from the men, the women with their children were locked in the church.

There they remained for three days, fed only bread and water. A friendly Turkish-Cypriot slipped them messages from their men, but he was caught and beaten, and the messages stopped coming. On the fourth day United Nations soldiers came in buses and took the women and children to refuge in the south. But the hundred or so men of their village remained behind. These are among the two thousand missing persons the Greek-Cypriot government says have never been accounted for by the Turks.

In spite of the years that had passed since the attack, she recalled the hour and the weather, the wind carrying the rumble of the guns, the batterings and threats and blows. She remembered the terror of the women, their pleas and prayers, as twilight darkened the church and some of them lit candles. She recalled the whimpering of the small children, the smells from the incontinent old women, the burdened passage of time until dawn.

The story took her an hour to relate, a grim and meticulous recital. Yet I could understand that for three years she had thought only of those days and nights, every sight and sound explored in her frantic hope that her husband might still be alive. Until, in the end, her grief and sorrow had knitted the memories into a dark spread that she clasped like a shroud.

By the time we reached the Stavros refugee camp it was hot and sunny, and the aluminum shed where the kindergarten class usually met was steaming. The teacher assembled the children on benches outside, shielded from the sun by a thatched roof.

The children, brought in by bus from one of the housing settlements, were a handsome flock, their dark eyes sparkling above their glowing cheeks. The girls were dressed in flowered frocks or jumpers, and the boys wore turtlenecks and shorts that exposed their tanned legs and nettle-scratched knees. They recited, argued, and wrestled with each other while the teacher made a valiant effort at discipline.

"Spring makes them restless," she apologized.

She called for some materials from the shed and a half-dozen children leaped forward, waving their hands to be chosen. An aggressive scamp in a maroon turtleneck offered his services in a hoarse, confident voice.

The teacher admonished him, "Christos, sit down."

When I took pictures during the playing of some makeshift musical instruments, Christos leaped forward again, obstructing the other children, mugging unabashedly for the camera.

"Christos, sit down!"

The children had made cut-outs of paper pigeons, addressed to the Turkish-Cypriot children across the Attila Line.

Deer Cypriot Turkish Children:

We, Greek children of "Mana" kindergarten in the refugee camp of Stavros, send greetings of love to you. We pray and hope that the pigeons of peace will remove the Attila Line and bring back peace, friendship and happiness to our beloved country, Cyprus.

The children held up their drawings of the island, of the sun and the mountains and their homes, while the class sang.

My little house,
My beloved house,
How I wish I could
Come back to you soon.

If I find you in ruins,
I'll rebuild you again,
I promise I will,
Little house that I love.

Once again Christos strutted forward, his voice growing louder. When another boy pushed him from behind in disgust, Christos whirled indignantly, small fists clenched and black eyes flashing.

"Christos, sit down!"

Giggling at his agitation and chagrin, the other children straggled through a few ragged bars, until their voices joined in unison again.

Another year has passed,
We are not yet in our homes,
But the flame to return
Burns on in our hearts.

For if we lived enslaved
We still hope and dream
For freedom to return
To our lovely Cyprus again.

Watching their vibrant faces, hearing their zestful voices singing the song of exile they might not really understand, I was stirred. Yet I could not help wondering if the laments of exile, the songs of estrangement, would not produce an irresistible momentum. As the children became young men and women, reminded ceaselessly of what had been lost, would they remain content with reciting poems and singing songs? Or, led by the bold and spirited Christos, would they be driven to regain by force what force had taken from them?

In this way generations pass to generations a chronicle of violence that compels violence, so stern and circumscribed a legacy that the young are unable to deviate from their deathward drift.

As Maria and I left the camp, the children sang:

Old year, hurry away now,
With your bitter memories.

A new year is coming,
And we will go home this year.

III

Sitting at a table in the darkened recesses of the Nicosia Taverna, Maria and I had dinner with Mando Meleagrou, daughter of the Cypriot novelist Eve Meleagrou, and of Dr. Ioannis Meleagrou. In a larger, adjoining room a wedding party was in progress, the guests erupting in laughter and toasts.

We ate *mezedakia,* the delicious assorted appetizers, and drank freely of the island's good wine. The girls recited the poetry of Cypriot poets, arguing amiably when they disagreed on their abilities. A few members of the wedding celebration formed a circle for an island dance, whirling like apparitions in the misted shadows.

During dinner I had noticed two young soldiers in United Nations uniforms at a table near our own, staring at Mando and Maria. As we waited for fruit and cheese, emboldened by wine, one of them came to our table. His face was flushed and he greeted us in fragmented English.

I motioned for him to sit down and he pulled out a chair. The other soldier stared stiffly away from us.

"Where are you from?" I asked.

The soldier grinned and shook his head.

Pointing to the girls, I said, "Cyprus." Then, tapping my chest, "America . . . United States." I gestured at him.

"Finland!" he said jubilantly and motioned at his companion. "Finland!"

We waved the other soldier to join us. He came timorously to take a chair at our table. We found he spoke no English at all.

Both youths appeared no older than nineteen or twenty, and extremely handsome, their blond hair and fair complexions radiating like miniature suns in the candled taverna.

"When will you go home?" I asked the youth who spoke some English.

"Home! Yes!" he nodded fervently. "Home . . ."

He smiled and winked at his friend as if to show he was making splendid progress.

"Yes, home!" he said. "Home . . . beautiful!"

He looked admiringly at the girls.

"Do you live near the mountains?" I asked.

"Mountains! Yes!" he said. "Mountains! Home!"

The other soldier permitted himself a guarded smile at Maria and Mando. We shared our fruit with them, toasting one another several times, utilizing gestures and laughter in place of speech. The bashful soldier began to smile with less painful shyness. When we rose, finally, to leave, both waved their disappointment.

"No! No! Please!"

"We have to go," Maria said firmly. "It is late."

I shook hands with them and Maria and Mando granted each one a final, warm smile. In that moment, I thought sadly, they were exiles too, young men set down between warring camps on an eastern Mediterranean island that must have seemed to them distant as the moon from their own northern homeland.

As we started for the door, I looked back one last time. The young soldiers stared after the girls with a wistful longing, not desire alone but simply a human need to share laughter, joy, and a promise of love.

On Sunday morning I was picked up by George Tsigarides of the Cyprus Tourism Organization. Tsigarides was also a refugee, one of the thousands of white-collar professionals who had fled from their homes, with perhaps a car and a few articles of clothing, during the 1974 invasion. We drove south. Along the coastal road from Limassol to Paphos, the majestic rocks and pounding surf reminded me of Monterey and Big Sur in California. We stopped briefly at some splendid tourist resorts and passed a number of spacious hotels under construction.

Tourism has always been an essential part of the island's economy. It accounted for 19 percent of the gross national product in 1972 and 23.8 percent in 1973, a year when 276,000 tourists visited the island. When the Turkish army invaded the northern area, 82 percent of the island's tourist accommodations were occupied. In 1975 tourism stood at only 5 percent of the GNP. Yet, so energetic and innovative have the Greek-Cypriots been in reviving the industry in the area left to them that some 180,000 tourists visited the south alone in 1976, and the 1977 total was expected to be close to the pre-invasion level.

Sitting in the sun-splashed terrace of a seaside hotel near Limassol, I considered the paradox of Cyprus. Tourists came to escape the stresses of their own lives. They had to be provided with tranquility, satisfying food, comfortable accommodations, recreation facilities, visits to antiquities.

No mention, in the travel folders, of refugee camps, or of villagers longing to return to their homes. Only the reminder that Cyprus offered the best travel and tourist buys in the sunny Mediterranean.

On a Tuesday morning, back in Nicosia, I crossed to the Turkish zone again. Husrev Suleyman was waiting for me, and we drove north. The churches we passed on the road to Kyrenia were locked for security reasons, Suleyman told me, the icons and other sacred artifacts removed and stored for safekeeping and a complete list submitted to the United Nations. The Greek-Cypriots I had spoken to claimed the churches had been looted, the religious objects shipped back to Turkey to be sold. All I could tell was that the exteriors were not damaged or defaced.

We paused at the lovely thirteenth-century Gothic cloister of Bellapais, once, a long time ago, called the Abbey of Peace. The monastery adjoined the village where Lawrence Durrell had lived and written *Bitter Lemons* in the early fifties, a fine and affectionate memoir of his years on Cyprus. The gardens about the Abbey were in luxuriant bloom, flowers ringing the trunks of fruit trees. Against a stunning sky, rooks cawed through the clear air above the cypresses that loomed like regal sentinels.

At Kyrenia the harbor was dominated by a seventh-century castle, which the British had used as a prison and which still had an aura of brooding menace. Beyond the castle, across the water, the Pentadaktylos mountains rose like a ghostly landscape out of the sea. From a row of brown and white houses with latticed windows edging the water came the lament of a Turkish song.

Later that day, after stopping for lunch at a roadside café where we ate kebab, a dish of spit-roasted lamb slices served with raw onions, tomatoes, and yogurt, we drove on and I asked Suleyman to stop at one of the villages I sighted off the main road.

The settlement had about a score of houses, ramshackle dwellings lining a dusty street. As we emerged from the car, a gaunt and mangy cat stared balefully at me and slipped away. A woman with a black scarf over her head appeared in a doorway, a barefooted child tugging at her skirt.

We crossed the street to a coffeehouse, a roofed porch occupied by about two dozen villagers, sitting at dilapidated tables. As we sat down at a table in a corner, some of the men stared at us curiously, while others avoided showing any interest. Their Turkish sounded gruff and guttural to me, accompanied by brusque motions of their hands. Most were older men, dark-skinned with wrinkled and weathered cheeks, dressed in shabby jackets, worn trousers, collarless shirts, caps and boots. A pair of men near us wore shoes without laces.

Suleyman took out a pack of cigarettes and offered it to a man at the table next to us. The man wiped his rough brown hands, with their ragged nails, on his trousers before accepting the pack. He pulled out a cigarette, lit it deftly, and grimaced with pleasure as a few wisps of smoke escaped from his nostrils.

Suleyman had told me that many of the older Turks spoke Greek, and I began speaking to them. The men answered a little stiffly in the beginning. Some among them reminded me of tuskless, aged bulls, slumped and withdrawn, with only an occasional flicker of the eyes to show that they were not asleep. Then, under prodding, one after another, the men began to talk.

They told me of the years of terror since 1955, when EOKA, the Greek-Cypriot guerrilla organization dedicated to winning "Enosis," union with Greece, by force, began its campaign of bombings and shootings. In 1958, 1963, 1964, 1967, one murderous eruption followed another. Even during periods of relative order, there were harassments, indignities, and cruelties perpetrated against them. One man told of trying three times to harvest his carob crop and three times being stopped and beaten by Greek-Cypriot bands. Another told of hauling a load of melons to market and being stopped by Greek auxiliary policemen, who, on the pretext of searching for hidden weapons, stabbed the fruit with their sticks, making a shambles of the load.

"Then they told me to take them to market," the old man's face trembled with fury. "After they ruined everything, they told me to take them to market!"

"Why would they do such a thing?" I asked.

"To torment us," said one man.

"Because they are devils," said another.

The young men sitting at the edge of the group watched us silently. The older Turkish-Cypriots had learned Greek during earlier, amicable periods. In later years, when conflict between the two communities increased, contacts were broken off and the young on each side were limited to their own language. If young Greek-Cypriots and Turkish-Cypriots could no longer talk to each other, I thought, what hope was there for the island they had to share?

"What is the main problem here?" I asked the older men again. They responded in brief, resentful phrases, one after the other:

"Union . . . always harping on union . . ."

"I don't want my family joined to Greece."

"We are Cypriots, but they have always thought of themselves as Greeks first."

"They never admit the island is our home, too."

"They hate us."

"Do you hate them?" I asked.

"Yes, I hate them!" exclaimed a man who had kept out of the conversation until then. "The only thing the filth understand is the sword!" He made a slashing gesture with his hand.

Several of the others protested, embarrassed by this show of bloodthirstiness before a stranger and guest. But when I asked if they could envisage living with Greek-Cypriots in mixed villages again, they shook their heads grimly, muttering objections and proscriptions. One hawk-featured old man with skin like flaking bark spoke for them all. "Does the mouse go to bed with the cat?"

Suleyman and I rose to leave. A hopelessness possessed me. As if to reassure me that he was not my enemy, the hawklike man rose and extended his hand, big fingers like raw, cracked knuckles. We clasped hands and I felt the gritty stone of his palm.

Then the other men rose, coming from their chairs and tables to crowd around me, extending their hands over the arms and shoulders of those in front. The young men, uncertain of the reason for the handclasps, joined in. For a flurried moment, shaking one hand after another, seeing the men threadbare and poor but persevering in their struggle to wrest a small yield from the land and from life, I felt an impassioned friendship for them all.

The pattern of that conversation was repeated at several other villages along the way. Some Turkish-Cypriots were less hostile than others toward the Greek-Cypriots, but most of them had embittered memories of being driven from their villages in the 1964 fighting. Those who sought to return after the cease-fire agreement of that time found their houses looted or burned, their fruit trees felled, their livestock stolen, and their wells filled in.

By the spring of 1964, all chance for reconciliation had been dissipated as the fighting between the two communities grew more intense. The outnumbered Turkish-Cypriots gathered for protection in fortified enclaves. Crowded together, denied access to their possessions and their land, dependent for utilities and services on Greek-Cypriots, they lived a wretched life. Those who chose to remain in their villages were at the mercy of Greek-Cypriot irregulars, whom even Archbishop Makarios could not control.

When I inquired about the long-term economic and social effects of partition, most of the villagers seemed unconcerned. They were interested only in survival, from one day to the next. A few hoped the time might arrive when some commerce and communication with the Greek-Cypriots in the south could be restored. But I did not meet a single Turkish-Cypriot who was willing to return to things as they were before the 1974 invasion.

The city of Famagusta. The street scenes, movements,

and sounds reminded me of a dozen Greek-island cities I had seen. Staring at the people, looking for characteristics that would identify them as Turks, I was struck by their resemblance to Greeks. They seemed the same sober old men and somber old women; young men in shirtsleeves; bare-legged young women in worn print frocks. Even a swarm of sun-browned children, shrieking and waving their thin arms like sticks in the air as they played, were disturbingly familiar.

The section of Famagusta surrounding the magnificent hotels whose reputation had once rivaled Miami Beach was cordoned off and guarded by soldiers. The owners and staff had fled during the 1974 invasion.

So for three years the once-teeming tourist complexes, their doors and windows shuttered, had lain like cast-aways—abandoned hulls picked clean as bones by the wind and sun. The sandy beaches below the balconies and pavilions, undisturbed except for the tide that lapped at the tracks of swallows and gulls, had become the silent playground of an eerie, dead preserve.

On the way back to Nicosia, Suleyman took me to the sites of three Turkish-Cypriot villages whose inhabitants, he said, had been murdered by Greek-Cypriots during the 1974 fighting. At each of the villages, Aloa, Maratha, and Sandallaris, a monument had been erected to the victims—more than two hundred names, all told, from a twenty-five-day-old baby to an eighty-nine-year-old woman.

I was suddenly resentful and suspicious. Were the memorials an elaborate façade to deceive journalists and tourists and to counteract the charges of Turkish atrocities that had been lodged by the European Commission on Human Rights? Finally, whether the monuments and graves were authentic or not, I mourned the names before me as a true memorial to all the innocent men, women, and children who had died on the island in the long and bloody years. Living together peacefully for extended periods, a time arrived when they became rapacious to butcher one another. Then, God help Moslem and Christian.

For generations, both sides have made accusations and protestations and offered explanations and rationales. None of these moldering arguments can obscure the iniquitous truth that, over the centuries, six times as many Greeks and Turks have been murdered by each other as the number— 500,000 Greek-Cypriots, 116,000 Turkish-Cypriots—that populate Cyprus today.

IV

Back in Nicosia, on the morning of my last day in Cyprus, walking up the stairway into an elegant sitting room, I met the stately and imposing Ethnarch, whose black-robed figure and bearded face were a familiar sight in newspapers across the world. He was not as tall as I had imagined him to be from the photographs, but he was strong-bodied, with a grave and courteous manner.

Archbishop Makarios had agreed to see me briefly despite his recent heart attack. He began our conversation by speaking about his illness, which had struck him while he was conducting an Easter mass in church. He had, he said, always been on guard against external foes, he had survived attempted assassinations, but he had never been ill, and this fluttering of the heart over which he had no control was an alien and disquieting experience. "I am not anxious for myself," he said quietly, "but for my people and for our Cyprus."

He had long proven his devotion and love for his people and his island. At the age of thirty-seven he was elected by popular vote to become the youngest archbishop in the history of the Church of Cyprus, and for thirty years he had guided his island's destiny. His struggle against colonialism, his exile by the British and his triumphant return in 1959, his stamina, courage, and faith had made him a deity for the Greek-Cypriots. As I had seen in the tents of refugees, in houses, shops, and offices, photographs of the archbishop shared the shrines of saints.

Yet, to the Turkish-Cypriots, the archbishop's shadow was ominous and omnipresent, every humiliation and pain they had to endure attributed to his personal direction.

I thought of some of these things as he talked to me of the island's suffering, the calamity of partition, his conviction that the island could not survive dismemberment. He spoke of the jubilation among the Greek-Cypriots the day President Carter was elected.

"I cannot describe to you what it was like," he said. "Our joy then because we thought that the president's campaign pledges, his assertions of friendship, his declarations on human rights and the justice of our cause, all would prove true. But now, with the United States endorsing a billion-dollar military aid program to Turkey, replacing the weapons and ammunition they used to kill our people, we feel betrayed."

I tried to suggest that disillusionment might be premature, that major powers tend to move slowly and along contradictory paths. After a moment, I hushed, feeling like a fool lecturing a king.

As I left the sun-splashed and tranquil sitting room, passing an adjoining room, I glimpsed, through a partially opened door, a white-jacketed attendant, perhaps a doctor, keeping vigil beside an oxygen tank.

(Soon afterward, back in America, hearing the news of the archbishop's death, I experienced a strange and pervasive sense of loss. I imagined the grief and devastation of his followers. I had asked one of them in Cyprus what the Greek-Cypriots would do if the archbishop died. He had answered, "We would pray.")

Departing for the airport later that afternoon, and my return flight to Athens, Maria and I were joined by an American-Cypriot writer and teacher, Tellos Kyriakides. We made a brief stop at a refugee camp in Larnaca. The camp, Maria told us, had just been settled a few months previously by refugees from the north. These were among the ten thousand or so Greek-Cypriots who had chosen to remain in their villages under guarantees of safety from the Turks after the 1974 invasion. Since then, according to word in Nicosia, they had undergone persecution, denial of medical services and lack of educational facilities for their children. All but two thousand of them had left their villages and were now refugees in the Greek-Cypriot zone. Maria was godparent to a child who had just been born a few weeks before in the Larnaca camp.

The mother, Flourenza, a small and sinewy woman of thirty-seven, led us into a hot, windowless shed. The infant had been sick for two weeks, she said, but now seemed better. We found the infant's swollen body covered with thick gray scales, overgrown with scabs. Shocked, we took the baby to the hospital in Larnaca. In the children's wing, a crowd of mothers and children jammed the doorway to the doctor's office. While Tellos and I waited outside, Maria and Flourenza carrying the baby, were taken directly inside. The doctor diagnosed the illness as a serious viral infection, often causing premature blindness if left untended. The baby would have to remain in the hospital for two to three weeks.

Flourenza seemed unable to relinquish the infant, until Maria, soothingly and consolingly, managed to separate them. After the nurse left with the baby, the mother stared after them, her hands raised stiffly and awkwardly to her breasts, as if still holding the child.

We drove her back to the camp and proceeded to the airport, riding in silence, the three of us aware, I think, that our chance visit to the camp may have prevented a child from going blind. That alone, I thought gratefully, was sufficient reason for my visit to Cyprus.

The writers of the old Greek tragedies have revealed to us that there is a wisdom which comes with suffering, a knowledge wrenched from sorrow. One does not have to be a king like Lear or Oedipus to enjoin this meaning. Greek-Cypriots and Turkish-Cypriots, villagers and townspeople, can come from their crucible to understand that while hatred and vengeance remain temptations, restraint and compassion can become their links to survive.

The people of Cyprus deserve to survive. I will never forget the old refugee farmer and his wife who were the first to say that families with children should have first call on the houses being built for the refugees; the women who retained their dignity and hospitality in the bleak, diminished surroundings of the camps; the Turkish-Cypriot farmers talking grimly of grievances and persecutions, and yet not allowing me—a Greek, in their eyes—to leave without shaking my hand; the man who wanted only his house, his patch of land and the graveyard where his dead are buried; the young Turkish-Cypriot guide Hassan describing Washington's dilemma in terms of a family problem; the lovely girl with her fearful memories, still working for a home and new life.

Greek-Cypriots and Turkish-Cypriots have lived together in harmony before, if not with the pristine affection some Greek-Cypriots now would have us believe existed. Before the colonial period, they had shared celebrations, and intermarriages were fairly common. The coming of the British, and then the Greek-Cypriot campaign for union created profound strains; still, for a long time, the two communities lived in peace and with tolerance for their differences. After the 1974 invasion, many Greek-Cypriots told of being befriended and protected by Turkish-Cypriots, sometimes hidden from mainland Turkish soldiers until they were able to escape. That awareness of their bond as Cypriots could help heal the wounds.

Perhaps the Cypriots will not be given a choice. From their sixteenth-century bondage, goaded by internal zealots, driven by external influence, their history has been a record of disorders. The proximity of the island to the rich oilfields of the Middle East suggests even greater pressure ahead. In the strident exchange of threats and claims over the Middle East, who will guarantee the independence and territorial integrity of Cyprus?

There is an old Greek-Cypriot proverb that if the stone falls on the egg, alas for the egg. If the egg falls on the stone, alas for the egg. Cyprus is the egg in an avalanche. Three years of partition may be only the beginning of a much longer displacement, as with the refugees of Palestine; these years may also be the mold for restless and uprooted generations, such as those that nourish internecine warfare in Northern Ireland. The prospects are gloomy and filled with foreboding.

My plane rose from the airport at Larnaca. An anthology of Greek-Cypriot poetry lay on my lap. I opened the book and reread some lines by Theodosis Pierides I had come across the night before:

> *I sing of the human beings who will come.*
> *I sing of the human beings who will have*
> *as nourishment in their lungs, our*
> *wide sky free—who will have*
> *all this soil of ours free*
> *for them to stride upon as masters.*
> *I sing of the human beings who will have*
> *much to reap each year,*

much to dance upon the threshing-grounds
and much to utter their joy,
in a thunderous voice, to sing of it.

A poet's faith defies hopelessness and gloom. Held that moment by his spirit, looking down on Cyprus, resplendent with its mountains, forests, orchards, and sea-washed coasts, seeing the land as it had been sculpted by God, man's partition invisible, I had a vision, momentary and yet compelling, of that night-haunted island redeemed by peace and light.

Death of the
Hotel Des Roses

AMONG THE fertile legends of Greece, there is a story that when he was dispensing islands to the other deities, Zeus neglected to provide one for Helios, the God of the Sun. Chagrined at his oversight, he caused a new lovely island to rise from the sea and gave it to Helios who named it Rodos, or Rhodes, after a beguiling nymph with whom he had fallen in love.

And truly it is a comely island. Hills and valleys are covered with lush forests of pine, oak, and cypress. Oleanders, mimosa, and bougainvillaea bloom around trellises, ascending the walls of houses, curling under the arches of bridges.

Outside the main city of Rhodes, across the span of this second largest of the Greek islands (majestic Crete is the first), there are the stunning gorges and rustic bridges, the redolent Valley of the Butterflies, the luxuriant forest of Mount Prophitis Ilias, and, most imposing of all, the magnificent temple of Athena overlooking the cerulean sea on three sides from the heights of the Acropolis of Lindos.

In June I spent a week on Rhodes, my third trip to that island in the last three years. Altho the throngs of summer tourists had not yet peaked, the city was packed. Each day the charter flights from Northern Europe poured out thousands of blond, fair-skinned men and women, who, stripping to the briefest of trunks and bikinis, emerged pale and nearly naked upon the beaches, where in the space of a few hours the intemperate sun burned them the shade of salmon. When twilight fell they retreated to the numerous hotels, vertical and horizontal hives sprouting along the water, multicolored in pallid imitation of the gardens and flowers. From each tiny balcony, in the rays of the setting sun, the wet suits and towels hung like thousands of pennants.

At night the streets of the city teemed with revelers, bouzouki music from the *tavernas* succumbing beneath the raucous rock music from discotheques. The cars swept by with a strident screeching of rubber and the shrill squealing of horns. Motorbikes whizzed along, driven by dark-haired, demonic young Greek centaurs, while hanging on behind were blond nymphs, their long golden hair streaming wild tendrils in their wake.

Among the conglomeration of new hotels which have sprung up in the city and along the beaches, the old Hotel Des Roses stands like an impassive relic of some grandiose past. A great, red-stoned mansion set within the splendor of its lush gardens. Inside the hotel, in an aura of shabby decorum and faded elegance, were vast, cavernous halls and huge bathrooms with the ancient plumbing strung together by fragments of wire. From the twelve-foot-high windows, between shimmering curtains which billowed inward like ghostly apparitions driven by winds from the sea, one looked down upon silent courtyards and pathways where decades before European nobility had walked in the fragrant gardens, while from a bandstand hidden in a sylvan grove, a chamber music ensemble played some serene and delicate melody.

The years have battered the Hotel Des Roses. Time has chipped its cornices, steps, and stones. In the frantic surge of building to accommodate the masses of tourists, the old hotel occupies too much land. The months ahead will see it razed, a dozen modern hotels erected on its great sprawl of land. But the gardeners still tend and care for the flowers with devotion, and the thick, colorful foliage conceals the crumbled planks of bandstand, the broken garden benches and fallen trellises.

The patrons who occupy the hotel are the same ones who have been coming each summer for years. Somehow they are lost within the vast halls and rooms. One sees them only at breakfast or at dinner, bloodless and emaciated characters in a De Sica or a Fellini movie, inbred aristocrats of some expiring line, their faces and fingers so pale and transparent, a strong gust of wind might blow them away.

In the great, columned dining hall they eat stiffly, silently, ordering food and wine in whispers so modulated they hardly stir the thin, fleshless line of their lips. In the afternoons one sees them sitting somberly on the terrace, impeccably attired in white suits, white shirts, white panama hats shading their parchment flesh from the sun, staring silently at the near-naked crowds that cluster on the beach or parade insouciantly along the walks.

For many years the long, fine stretch of beach had been the exclusive property of the Hotel Des Roses. But the need for space had overcome its privacy. In April of this year, foreshadowing the demolition of the hotel, the beach had been rented to concessionaires, who set up hundreds of brightly colored new umbrellas and lounge chairs for which they charged fifteen drachmas (fifty cents) a day.

All that remained for the Hotel Des Roses, still subject to the daily fee, was a narrow stretch of beach directly before the hotel. In this space were packed perhaps fifty faded umbrellas that had seen service for many years and perhaps double that number of rickety lounge chairs, all managed and looked after by a Greek named Leonidas.

He was a big, handsome man, perhaps in his middle or late fifties, his skin shaded a deep, dusky brown by the sun. All I ever saw him wear was a pair of faded, blue trunks, a short-sleeved, white terrycloth jacket, and a small, white sea captain's cap.

The beach of the Hotel Des Roses had been his responsibility for almost fifteen years and before I had heard him put his feelings into words, I sensed his detachment from the changes that time had wrought. As people entered his patch of sand looking for a place to settle, he would deftly open an umbrella and set up chairs for them. To those coming onto the beach for the first time, he would courteously explain the fifteen-drachma charge, overcoming their resentment by his dignity, by a wry shrug and ex-

pressive movement of his fingers that allowed them to share
the irony of asking people fifteen drachmas for the sun and
the sea, without offering at the least a simple tent or bath-
house where they might change. Afterwards he'd plod back
to one of his posts, jingling the change in the pocket of his
jacket, looking at the water while around him people struggled under loosely held towels or robes to slip out of wet
trunks, the little pale triangle of their buttocks gleaming
white within the areas of flesh burned and darkened by the
sun.

In the hours each day I spent on the beach, I watched
the crowds at rest and at play. I came to admire the way
Leonidas did his job, the aura of dignity about him. I never
saw him hurried, ruffled, or bad-tempered. With the old patrons from the hotel who came to sit gingerly under an umbrella, he was grave and restrained. With the young sports
who gathered on the beach, he indulged in a teasing banter.
They sparred and jested around him like young steers
around a grizzled old bull they respected. When they
whined or complained of their lot, Leonidas derided them
vigorously.

"You have your wind, a good heart and your youth . . .
what are you crying about? Stop dreaming of a rich, blond
girl who will support you and go to work and sleep in
peace."

Sometimes he would be joined by a group of old waiters and chefs from the neighboring hotels, a group of acerbic old men resembling an ancient Greek chorus. They
would make caustic, derogatory remarks in Greek about the
people cluttering the city and the beach. "*E xeni*—the

strangers," they called them in derision. But Leonidas defended the tourists.

"They come in good faith for the sun and the beauty of the island," I heard him say once. "It's not their fault there are so many of them they change the island and the people."

"Whose fault is it, then?" an old gray-haired waiter asked. "Are we to blame? The government? God? Who is to blame?"

Leonidas stared across the plain of umbrellas, at the thousands packed and crowded on the beach. In that moment from my vantage point a dozen feet away, I found myself straining for his answer.

All he said was, "I don't know."

In the week I spent on Rhodes, when I was not basking in the sun on the beach, I crossed the island by car to visit my friends, Will and Mavis Manus, who lived in Lindos. I climbed again the steps to the Temple of Athena, and standing on the crest of the mountain, looked with awe and pleasure across the vast, limitless panorama of water, one of the loveliest sights in all of Greece, matching the gorges of Delphi, the pine forests of Arcadia, the white mountains of Crete. As I descended I passed long, ragged lines of tourists ascending, pausing wearily to get their breath, measuring how far they had come, how distant the peak remained. And all along their route were the stands and shops and encampments of the women imploring them to buy fabrics and shawls and souvenirs.

In the evening, after the last of the tour buses had departed, the stone steps to the Acropolis deserted in the darkness, I sat in one of the *tavernas* with my friends. We drank the good dry red wine of Rhodes and they told me of changes taking place in the town of Lindos. The citizens had a higher standard of living and more possessions than they had been able to afford before, but these had been achieved only by their frantic efforts to capture their share of the money the tourists were bringing in. Unable to rest while prodded by the thought they were missing hundreds of tourists, they had begun to omit their siestas during the fierce heat of the afternoon. There were reports of more illnesses of various kinds. At the least, missing their rest produced a general bad temper. Again, the carpenters and stonemasons had abandoned their trades because more money could be made photographing tourists ascending and descending the Acropolis by donkeys.

"Will they return to their trades when the season is over?" I asked.

"They will sit in the *tavernas* waiting for the summer," one of my friends said. "The women will stay home and crochet and knit to get ready for next season."

And there had not been a wedding in the town for almost two years. Courting a girl from a Greek town family was too burdensome a task for a young Greek male when he had ample numbers of eager foreign girls to occupy his attention. When he had philandered thru a series of these girls, he gained a stigma among the families of the town, so that even if he and a town girl decided to marry, the family might not find him acceptable. So the young girls pined and the young men fled to find their fortunes elsewhere. And on

Lindos, as in all of Greece, all who would someday be left were the old men and old women and a scattering of children waiting to leave when it was their time to go.

On my last day in Rhodes, returning from the beach at noon to the Hotel Des Roses, I saw a group of four or five hundred people gathered before the hotel, one of the excursions off the cruise ships that anchored in the harbor of the island for the day. As an entertainment provided for them after eating lunch, a colorfully costumed troupe of Greek men and women had gathered around a lyre player in the old stone courtyard. Wearing heavy woolen jackets and trousers, ankle-length skirts and boots, they danced under the blazing and relentless midday sun, sweat pouring down their faces, while around them hundreds of cameras hissed and clicked.

I could not help a feeling of sadness as I watched them. Once they had danced on their feastdays, dances to celebrate the harvest, the blessings of bread and wine, the birth of a child, the marriage of a son—dances that nourished their spirits and reaffirmed the sense of their past.

Now, posturing and grimacing like absurd marionettes, they danced a graceless, joyless parody of celebration, mimicking bravado and gusto as the shutters snapped and the tourists whistled and applauded.

Starting to leave, I noticed Leonidas, who had come from the beach and stood on the perimeter of the crowd. I moved toward him, planning to speak to him, to tell him good-by because I was not sure I would see him again. But he was intent on watching the dancers. As I came near him

I saw an expression of such pity and despair on his face that I could not bear for him to see me, and turned quickly away.

Later that afternoon, I waited on the terrace of the Hotel Des Roses for a taxi that would drive me to the airport. Across the sea, rain was falling on the village of Marmaris on the mainland of Turkey, and the masses of black and menacing clouds were surging toward us.

Under the threat of rain, so rare an occurrence in summer, the beach had deserted, almost all of the chairs emptied of their occupants except for a few stragglers still gathering their possessions. Along the far stretches of sand the attendants gathered their umbrellas, carrying them to be stacked and tied down beneath the canvases. In the compound before the Hotel Des Roses, Leonidas folded down his umbrellas and his chairs.

The scene was an eerie and beautiful one, the sky darkening, the water turning choppy, the thunder rumbling closer. Against the black, seething waves I could still see the small white cap of Leonidas moving back and forth.

A chilled wind touched my neck and I shivered and looked up. Above my head the great battlements of the old hotel were shrouded in a darkening mist. On one of the upper floors they were closing the shutters with a loud banging of wood. Beyond the red stone cornices, lightning flashed, a jagged line cutting the sky. The first drops of rain began to fall.

I rose and started to move inside. When I looked back once before entering the door, Leonidas was gone; all that remained on the deserted expanse of beach were the stacks of umbrellas and chairs covered by canvas. One edge of a canvas had torn loose in the wind and it rose into the air, fluttering vainly back and forth, like the ancient, ragged, and solitary ensign of some vanquished and departed host.

An Easter Odyssey

![decoration] ON OUR Olympic Airways flight from Athens to Rethymnon, Crete, I sat on the aisle in a three-seat row, my wife, Diana, in the middle seat beside me. The window seat was occupied by a white-haired, wiry old man with several well-filled K-Mart shopping bags at his knees. He told us he was a widower returning from one of his periodic visits to America with gifts for his grandchildren. We told him we were visiting Crete for the first time to spend Easter with relatives we had never seen before. The old man wiped a tear from his eye and wished us well.

A short while later we began our descent toward the port city of Rethymnon. As the swirling clouds cleared and we glimpsed the ground, a murmur of awe and delight rose from the passengers at the windows. The old man motioned us to his window. I looked down at my first sight of Crete, the birthplace of my father and mother. Clearly visible in the midst of Homer's wine-dark sea, the island was a dazzling and radiant panorama of flowers.

"The garden of Crete . . ." the old man whispered and fervently made the sign of the cross.

The garden of Crete. . . . Once, in a memory from my childhood, I heard the island referred to in that way. When spring arrived in Crete, my mother told me, it was as if the island were a spacious garden bursting with flowers.

My mother, Stella Christoulakis, was born in the village of Nipos, in the western part of the island near Khania. My father, the Reverend Mark Petrakis, came from the village of Argyroupolis in the mountains above Rethymnon. In 1916, my parents emigrated from Crete to America, where my father had been assigned as a priest to a parish of young Cretan coal miners in Price, Utah. They brought with them four of my brothers and sisters.

I have in my possession a faded, treasured photograph taken of my family in Crete about the time they began their journey to America. My father wears a tall, black stovepipe hat common to Greek Orthodox priests of the period, a long, black cassock mantling him from throat to ankles. My mother, a small comely woman with thick, long hair braided and then tied up into a bun, stands beside him. My two brothers and two sisters, ranging in age from six to twelve, cluster around them.

The family remained in Utah until my father was reassigned to a parish in Savannah, Georgia. A few years later they moved to St. Louis, Missouri, where I was born. That same year they made a final move to Chicago, where the last child in our family, another sister, was born.

Now, as our flight descended toward Cretan soil, I recalled how the constellations of my childhood glittered with stories of that tragic and lovely island. The songs, tales, and proverbs of Crete passed from my parents to me. Although I had been born in America, I had always felt a part of me belonged to that faraway land.

Gorgios, the young taxi driver we hired at the airport, drove us through a tangle of cars, bicycles, and motorbikes that clogged the streets of Rethymnon. On the sidewalks, crowds milled about the stalls of peddlers selling vegetables and fruit. In outdoor cafés people sat and sipped coffee and drank small glasses of *ouzo* and *raki.*

Along with black headbands, Cretan men wore the *vraka* or black baggy pants, that swirled around their black boots as they walked. In the sash of their waistbands, some carried ivory-handled daggers inlaid with silver.

They stared at us as the taxi passed, realizing we were strangers. Their expressions were wary, sometimes even hostile. The centuries of slavery and war the Cretans have endured and the devastating occupation of the island by German troops after the Battle of Crete in the Second World War have left the islanders resentful and rebellious. Cretans, my father told me, make staunch friends and unrelenting enemies.

We left the city, the road winding up into the majestic mountain ranges that run the length of the island. To the west were the *Levka Óri* (White Mountains). In the center of the island was Mount Ida. To the east was the Dhíkti range where Zeus, ruler of the heavens and father of other gods, was born.

Aside from their stark imposing beauty, the mountains affected the island's history by isolating regions and villages and by setting up a natural barrier against invaders.

Above the peaks of the highest mountains was the glowing sun, radiating a light that Greek writers from the ancient dramatists to the modern poets sought to describe.

When words could not capture its resplendence, they assigned the sun the attributes of a god and worshiped it. The warrior Ajax, about to perish in battle, cried out to die in the light. When the painter El Greco left Crete for Spain, the skies he painted retained the luminous light above the island he had left behind.

Then there were the flowers. Viewing them from the height of the plane was an enchanting spectacle. But to see them close was to have our senses overwhelmed.

Flowers curled across stone walls, adorned the small whitewashed churches on the slopes of the mountains, trailed along the trellises of houses, bloomed from window boxes, softened the spiked plants and thorny bushes. Their aroma filled the air with a dizzying fragrance of carnations and bougainvillea.

Meanwhile, whatever mountain road we traveled, we were never out of sight of the sea for long. The water would be hidden for a few moments and then as the taxi veered around a precipitous cliff of rock, the sea came stunningly into view, an expanse of turquoise-blue water stretching toward the horizon.

But the tranquil surface of the sea was deceptive. From the time of the ancient Greeks, beneath the placid waters lay the wrecks of sunken ships and the ruins of lost cities.

Twilight had fallen as we drove slowly into Argyroupolis, on the surface resembling so many other villages we already had passed. Chickens clucked and scurried to escape the wheels of the auto. A few dogs barked. People hurried from their houses to herald our arrival. All the villagers had been waiting and they greeted us with buoyant cries of *"Kalos Orisate!"* "Welcome! Welcome!"

A small group of children ran to my uncle's house to let the family know we had arrived. As we emerged from the taxi, our first cousins Antonia and Yannis Couides and their daughters, Eleni and Melpa, came from the house to greet us.

How fulfilling it was to embrace relatives we had never seen before but that we felt instantly we knew. Perhaps it was the cards, letters, and snapshots sent back and forth across the ocean for years. Perhaps it was the resemblances to family members in America. As we hugged, laughing and talking at the same time, the villagers clustered around us, sharing the jubilation of the reunion as though they were related to us as well.

I asked about my uncle, Father Joseph, Antonia's father. She told us he had been anxiously awaiting our arrival all day and she had finally prevailed upon him to rest. He was asleep in his bed in the kitchen.

As we entered the house, the old priest woke with a start. He scrambled from the bed, his countenance anxious and apprehensive, as if he feared our arrival was a dream that would escape him once he woke. Then he raised his arms to embrace me fervently.

Father Joseph was in his middle eighties with a strong, stocky body. He had snow-white hair and a white beard. In America he would have made an authentic St. Nick.

Although he had been retired from his parish church

for almost ten years—another priest serving in his place—in honor of our visit he planned to participate in the liturgy that evening.

Now he tugged at my arm, asking me to accompany him to church so he could prepare for the service. Diana, with Antonia, Yannis, and their daughters, would follow later.

The church was located in the lower village and to get there we had to descend about a hundred stone steps. Although the curve of the sky gleamed with stars, the night was pitch black. Father Joseph told me he had been descending and ascending those steps all his life but I still marveled at how confidently he skipped down, as agile and surefooted as a mountain goat. Uncertain of my own footing, I kept falling behind until Father Joseph returned for me and took my arm and led me carefully and safely down the stairs.

When we entered the small village church, only a few somber old men and old women waited silently before the icons. After Father Joseph introduced me to Father Stavros, a dark-haired, dark-bearded young priest, he led me to an alcove occupied by Barba Leontis, a lean old *psalti* or cantor, wearing a faded, black cassock that hung loosely on his gaunt frame. Father Joseph introduced me as his nephew from America and asked Barba Leontis to allow me to sit beside him.

The first parishioners began to arrive, strong, sun-darkened men and women, dressed in their best clothing. The lovely girls and handsome boys had well-scrubbed faces and necks. A row of old patriarchs, stiff-necked as roosters, took their places against the wall. A coven of black-garbed old women loomed like tragic figures in an ancient chorus. A black-haired beauty, exquisite as Helen of Troy, entered church with the regal walk of a princess.

Many of their faces reminded me of parishioners from my father's parish in Chicago. I stared at them, shaken at the resemblances, so precise that I was able to affix names from my past to many of them.

The services began. Father Joseph emerged from the sanctuary to make the sign of the cross over the congregation.

He wore scarlet and gold vestments I remembered had once belonged to my father. As the vestments grew worn, my mother sent them to Father Joseph and he wore them for years. He looked toward me and when he saw that I recognized the vestments, his face flashed an endearing smile.

Beside me, Barba Leontis began to chant one of the old Byzantine hymns, and on the opposite side of the church, two young cantors who had taken up positions across from us intoned a response. The old cantor's voice was husky and grating, while the voices of the young cantors were strong and clear.

At an early point in the liturgy, Barba Leontis grasped my arm and pointed to the hymnal. "Sing," he said to me in a low, urgent voice.

I stared at him in shock. He must have mistakenly thought that Father Joseph had brought me to sit beside him because I was also a cantor from America. I struggled to explain that I had never been a cantor, only an altar boy.

The old man attributed my stammering explanation to some modesty with which he had scant patience. He once more sternly admonished me to "Sing!" His voice had risen and from below us in the church, a number of parishioners stared up at us.

Throwing prudence to the winds, drawing on memories of my father's church and its hymns, in a low, nervous voice, I started to chant the music. The young cantors grimaced and sneered. Barba Leontis glared at them and urged me on.

Father Stavros and Father Joseph joined voices in chanting the liturgy, the cantors responding. I moved closer to the hymn book, struggling to decipher words and music, trying to imitate Barba Leontis. No one in the church seemed to understand that I hardly knew what I was doing, so my confidence grew and my voice became stronger. I felt possessed suddenly of an awesome Cretan force and power.

At a moment when my voice resonated robustly across the church, my wife, Diana, Antonia, Yannis, and their daughters entered the church. Diana heard my voice before she saw me and across the distance that separated us, I witnessed her shock. She had never heard me sing in church before and she must have thought it an Easter miracle. She bent her head, and quickly made the sign of the cross. Beside her Yannis beamed at me proudly.

I had experienced many Easters as a child, then as a youth and an adult. But none of them equalled the beauty and emotion of that Easter night in the village in Crete. I felt bound in some irrevocable way to the villagers. The church, candles, incense, the beloved face of my uncle and the stern countenance of the young priest, all fused with my past. I felt, as well, the mystical presence of the night that loomed around us, sky, earth, and water linking the present to the mythic past.

At midnight when the lights were extinguished and the church was hurled into darkness, I waited, trembling with an excitement and anticipation I had not felt since childhood. Father Joseph emerged from the sanctuary holding the first candle, its frail light glinting across his white beard. From that solitary candle other candles were lighted and flared into flame until several hundred candles gleamed like stars on the waves of night.

When it came time to express the salutation, "*Christos Anesti!*" "Christ is Risen!" I felt the words bursting from my soul, "*Christos Anesti!*" I cried to Barba Leontis. "*Alithos Anesti!*" "Truly, He is Risen!" his hoarse voice cried in response.

When we emerged from the church at the end of the liturgy, the night glittered with numerous fires as villagers in surrounding mountain villages burned great bonfires engulfing effigies of Judas. The night also cracked and echoed with the thunder of hundreds of guns being fired in celebration.

We ascended the steps toward the upper village, Antonia and the girls holding their flickering candles. In the house we sat down to the festive Easter dinner that concluded the forty days of fasting. I was given the baked lamb's head as a special delicacy, which I was unable to eat. After several futile attempts to convince me what a treat it was, Father Joseph gave up and attacked it with gusto, grinning at me, savoring every bite while little specks of lamb's eyes glittered in his beard.

Sated with food, Diana and I were given the principal bed, belonging to Yannis and Antonia. It had been built by my great-grandfather in the previous century. For more than a hundred years it had provided a haven for family births and deaths. My father had been born in the bed and my grandparents died in the bed that symbolized the continuity of the family.

I slept restlessly for a while and woke to a light rain striking the roof. I imagined my father as a boy listening to the rain. I rose then and made my way outside to stand on the porch. The earth around me was silent and shadowed, the first frail light breaking over the monoliths of mountains. In that moment I witnessed the dawn in a way I had never experienced it before, the night not yet relinquishing its power, the day not yet gaining ascendancy. Darkness and light played out an ancient drama of confrontation before my eyes. Finally, wearily, I returned to bed and slept.

In the morning I woke to the pealing of countless bells. They rang in Argyroupolis and resounded from numerous other villages. We ate bread and cheese and drank warm milk to their pealings and echoes.

When the young taxi driver, Gorgios, returned to take us back to the airport in Rethymnon, our family and most of the villagers gathered to bid us farewell. I embraced my cousins and the children, wondering with melancholy, when I would ever see them again. Yet I was grateful at how much intimacy and love had been fostered in the space of a single night.

The last person to whom I said good-by was Father Joseph. The old man held me at arm's length for a long time, staring into my face as if to memorize every bone and strip of flesh, because he understood we probably never would see each other again. Then he drew me slowly, breathlessly, into his arms. As he hugged me tight, I smelled the scents of incense and candle wax on his cassock and felt the trembling of his flesh. Finally, he whispered a blessing for our safe journey home and hugged me one last time.

We climbed into the taxi, carrying the parcels of bread, cheese, and the container of olive oil they pressed upon us. When we started to drive slowly away, the villagers began to wave. Father Joseph raised his hand one last time, as if beseeching us to remain. As the taxi started down the road, a small band of children ran alongside. They escorted us through the village, scattering the chickens, agitating the dogs. When the children could no longer keep up, they stopped and waved their hands vigorously and cried their final farewells.

As we drove deeper into the mountains, their shrill young voices carried in melodious cries across the morning. We could still hear their voices and the distant, pealing bells of Crete long after the village was lost to our sight.

Notes from an
English Journey

ON OUR British Airways flight from Chicago to London, I vainly courted sleep. When I finally managed to doze, my dreams rode comet's tails, images deflected by an attendant's shadow or by the loss of darkness swiftly becoming sunrise. Arriving at Heathrow Airport, we taxied toward the gate and waited. The sonorous voice of our captain explained the delay.

"The buses are here below us, ladies and gentlemen, but we cannot get you off because we haven't any steps. I am, however, reliably informed by staff that they're looking most diligently for steps."

The steps arrived and we descended from the plane. As we boarded the buses, the Boeing 747 loomed above us like some massive sculpture that would remain affixed forever to the Earth. Emerging from the buses in the custom's area, we had our passports stamped and entered one of the gleaming black Austin taxis. Through snarls of traffic our patient driver delivered us to the Bedford Hotel in Bloomsbury.

At first sight the hotel perched directly above the noisy, teeming street wasn't reassuring. I expected the sounds of traffic clamoring into a room the size of a linen closet with a communal bath down the hall. We entered the lobby and registered and the desk clerk rang her bell. A tall, white-haired bellman named Mr. Napier led us up the lift to the third floor. He unlocked our room door with the demeanor of a magician about to unveil a rabbit. The room on the rear of the hotel was a delightful surprise with three windows overlooking a garden refulgent with early June flowers. Red and yellow petals adorned a small stone fountain in which a spout of water rippled and splashed.

"You'll find this restful indeed," Mr. Napier said.

And, indeed, for a while we rested.

Taking our first walk in London later that afternoon, the day was a sun-suffused splendor. As if bewitched by the warmth and brightness, men and women with their shoes and stockings removed and their sleeves rolled up, lounged on the grass in Bloomsbury Square. We passed through the gate, which bore the injunction "Dogs Must Not Foul Upon This Open Square." I imagined some canine tourist, freed from the leash, scampering toward that verdant oasis and then braking in panic before that stern admonition.

Making a circle of the square, we passed the parish church of St. George, built in 1720–1730 by the architect Nicholas Hawksmoor. The plaque before the church read:

"Scene of the Bloomsburg christening in Dickens. An-thony Trollope novelist and Richard Benson, founder of the Cowley Fathers were baptised and, the parents of Sidney Smith, the wit, were married here."

Pausing for a moment, I wished for an additional line or two offering evidence of the wit of Sidney Smith. Unknown to me, he might have been the Don Rickles or Bob Hope of his time.

The next morning we walked down Southhampton Row, following Victoria Embankment along the Thames. The day was as warm and glowing as the previous one had been, the excursion ships on the river jammed with people. Tour buses swept along the thoroughfare, bicyclists darting like terriers around them.

Around the houses of Parliament the crowds grew denser. From a church where a wedding had just ended, men in formal hats and cutaways and women in shimmering gowns, resembling characters from *Brideshead Revisited*, emerged into the courtyard. They gathered in smiling and chatting groups, unperturbed by the gawking of tourists wearing shorts and jerseys emblazoned with the names Milwaukee, Detroit, Cleveland, Chicago.

After sunlight, the interior of Westminster Abbey, the most famous church in the English-speaking world, was dismal. That gloomy ambience was deepened by the numerous catafalques, memorial tablets, chapels, and tombs.

In the poet's corner of the Abbey were a number of memorials. Dylan Thomas, whose magnificent voice graced his poems, is buried at Laugharne, but his tablet offers one lovely line, "Time held me green and dying while I sang in my chains like the sea."

Alfred Lord Byron died in 1824 in the Greek struggle for independence against the Turks. He was thirty-six years old and the lines on his tablet divine his spirit: "But there is that within me which shall tire Torture and Time and breathe when I expire."

On and on through the abbey, from one chapel to another crypt, tombs of soldiers from warrior lineages dating back to William the Conqueror and the Lion-Hearted Richard. Their births and deaths recorded by families so generations of visitors might pause and read their names. Perhaps absorb, as well, that warning carried from the dead to the living.

"Reader, who ere thou art, let the sight of this tombe imprint in thy mind that young and old [without distinction] leave this world and fail not to secure the next."

Emerging from the abbey, I gratefully inhaled the sunshine and air. I felt then, an impression reaffirmed through visiting other imposing cathedrals, that I haven't any fondness for those edifices poking their ornate spires into the heavens. They seem built less as places to worship God than as places to worship Man. As if mortals, uncertain what space they might be apportioned in paradise, created venerable memorials to their pride and vanity on Earth.

We joined Felicity Glen and Delia Cooke, editors at Severn House Publishers, for afternoon tea at Brown's Hotel, the quintessentially English hostelry founded by Brown, one of Lord Byron's valets. Tea in America involved a nondescript tea bag dunked into hot water. But English tea is as elegant as a minor coronation. Since reservations weren't accepted, we had to queue for a while, close to an American woman who said plaintively to her companion, "All my life I've wanted to have tea in Brown's." If Mr.

Napier, our gracious bellman, had been there, I imagined him saying, "Madame, you will have your tea."

She had her tea and so did we, seated on plush sofas in the paneled, luxurious lounge. The tea, served by formally dressed waiters, was fragrant leaves brewed in a silver pot and strained as it was poured. There were also three-tiered trays of finger sandwiches, cropped slices of dark and light breads enclosing moist meats, watercress, and cheese. There were, finally, delicious scones, hot English biscuits garlanded with buttery cream and strawberry jam. Departing, regretfully, after two hours, I felt I would never be able to hoist an ordinary tea bag again without dismay and disdain.

From King's Cross station on our way to York, we sat on the train across from a handsome, bronzed older couple from Denmark. They were proud to be able to speak to us in our native tongue. Our conversation was joined by a half-dozen people, including a Liverpool bus driver, a policeman on holiday, and a couple from Newcastle. Their voices were wry, jovial, witty, and cheerful. They evidenced the same zest and friendliness we found later in English taxi drivers, news vendors, chambermaids, and barmen. With the English temperament as volatile and voluble as that of Greeks, two weeks in England convinced me that Zorba would have found himself totally at home in the Boar's Head Pub.

In York we lunched in an old sporting club with Canon Ralph Mayland of the Minster. In an eerily silent room curiously detached from the bustling streets of the city, the canon told us of the fierce storm on the night of July 9,

1984, when lightning struck the cathedral. By the mighty efforts of fire brigades that came from a radius of twenty miles, the fire was contained except for the south transept (one of the lateral arms of a cruciform church), which was sorely damaged.

To allow us to view the extensive renovation that had been going on since that night (donning hard hats and signing waivers of liability) we climbed the 101 steps inside the stone stairwell. When we emerged just below the dome, through the railings of the scaffolding the swarms of tourists looked like tiny toy figures in the nave of the cathedral far below. The moment was wondrous, dizzying and frightening, returning me to some myth of childhood when I conceived of a divine creator building heaven and Earth and, finally, fashioning human beings.

Returning to London late that afternoon, we ate dinner in the buffet car, lingering over our cups of dark, strong coffee. Through the train window the setting sun crimsoned the brick farmhouses and barns and tinted the foliage of trees. Remembering similar landscapes while driving to college lectures across Ohio, Illinois, Kansas, and Wisconsin, I thought English farmers probably had more in common with American farmers than they did with their countrymen in London and Manchester. Like farmers in America, many of them spent their lives working land on which their parents had lived. After marrying and raising their families, they would be buried, finally, in cemeteries not far from the houses where they had been born. Frequent travelers to foreign lands might consider such an existence restricted, but the quality of life isn't determined by the miles one covers.

Among Edgar Allan Poe's conditions for happiness (fulfilling labor, life in the open air, the love of another human being) there wasn't any mention of travel.

Paddington Station was farther from Bloomsbury than King's Cross and we arrived there by taxi the following morning to find all trains delayed because of electrical storms that affected the signals and switches. People pushing carts of luggage assembled tensely beneath a huge departures board that listed a score of trains. From time to time the numerals and letters whirled, blurred, and clicked into place announcing a gate. Then a phalanx of waiting passengers leaped forward, charging to the train.

Our train did not yet have a gate listed and I waited as anxiously as a runner at the block, not wishing to be left behind. Fascinated at the way the rotating numerals resembled giant Las Vegas slot machines, I didn't notice our train being posted. My wife nudged me several times before I emerged from my trance. By then, to my dismay, a hundred passengers had stampeded to the gate before us.

Touring several of the colleges of Oxford, I found it difficult to separate the beauty and aura of tradition that existed about each of them. They were different in size but similar in the great paneled commons rooms and the shadowed tranquility of the chapels. We were there during examination week and to anyone accustomed to the casual attire of American students, it was startling to see a formally dressed young man bicycling through the cobbled streets, his black gown flying behind him.

Walking from Christ Church to New College, we passed the house where Edmund Halley of Halley's Comet had maintained his observatory while teaching at Oxford between 1703 and 1742. In a nearby cloister was a door bearing the austere warning "Do Not Ring Unless An Answer Is Required." I was tempted to press the bell and when someone opened the door, inquire, "What is Truth?" But as a stranger in the city, I did not wish to be accused of frivolity.

In the commodious dining room of New College, the long tables were set for dinner, the lamps glowing across the silverware and crystal. A stillness hung over the room, a silence that belonged to the floor of the sea, yet that could be shattered in an instant by the onslaught of several hundred boisterous young men resembling the swift gladiators in the film *Chariots of Fire*.

The walls of the room were decorated with ornately framed paintings of former students who had distinguished themselves in their professions of law, politics and war. There were portraits with dates as early as the fourteenth century, and memorials to the soldiers who had died in their country's wars. One felt the ghosts of the generations of young men who had dined in this room, radiating life, health and the force of dreams.

Departing New College, in a broad expanse of green grass, a barefooted girl lay on her stomach, intently reading a book. Her long golden hair streamed down her back and shimmered in the sun. I wondered if she were conscious of the stunning idyll she made, perhaps evoking desire in young men and a nostalgia for a still unforgotten springtime in older men. Curious, also, as to what she was reading, I did not have the temerity to disturb her to ask whether the book was Byron, Shelley, or Germaine Greer.

Later that day, traveling from Oxford to Bristol required we twice transfer trains. The sky had begun to darken with swirling clouds foreshadowing a storm. On the final leg of the journey we occupied a compartment with three men. One was a young man dressed in a dark suit, white shirt, and tie, holding an open attaché case on his knees. The second had long sideburns and drowsy eyes. The third man was gray-haired, and he was earnestly reading abook whose title I noticed was *Greek Mythology*.

Except for the rumbling of the wheels and the lurching of the car racing along the tracks, a somber silence prevailed in the compartment, a reserve markedly different from the conviviality of the train journey we had taken to York. I wondered if it were a matter of class or simply closer confinement. Diana and I spoke briefly but our voices seemed obtrusive in the compartment and we fell silent.

Meanwhile, the storm clouds had compressed into darker masses and then the rain began. Falling lightly at first, it became a downpour, lashing the windows with such force that the landscape was totally obscured.

Inside our compartment the young man kept studying his papers, the man with long sideburns dozed, and the older man kept reading his book.

In Bristol we were taken into the care of silver-haired, gracious Angus Sinclair, who was a graduate of New College and who represented the Central Office of Information in Bristol. We drove with him from Bristol to Bath, the old Roman city where the annual Bath Festival was in progress. We had lunch with festival chairman Simon Buchanan and Sam Hunt, assistant curator of museums. Buchanan was a big, robust man who unabashedly boosted the festival of concerts, art exhibits, and plays as "the greatest festival in all England!"

After lunch Sam Hunt toured us through the Spa. We drank a glass of the water that tasted rather like warm Alka Seltzer with a sharp saline aftertaste that has to be therapeutic for the system because there wasn't any other reason to drink it. Sam Hunt led us through the old Roman catacombs, past the displays of antiquities. Each time we paused, his quiet, informed voice drew a cluster of tourists who pressed closer to hear his words.

Returning to London, we had dinner (we were, it is true, forever eating) with Lionel Carley, director of the Overseas Visitor's Information Services of the C.O.I., and Julian Critchley, a member of Parliament for Aldershot. Both men were also distinguished writers, Carley for a biography of the composer Delius, and Critchley for a number of books, including his autobiography, *Westminster Blues*. They talked perceptively about the Common Market, Greece and Turkey in NATO, the policies of Reagan and Thatcher. Yet I most clearly remember a recollection by Critchley of his student days at Oxford. Warned by his father not to pass his summers in indolence, he worked as a driver and guide for Americans touring Europe. He recalled most pervasively the summer he had driven four young American girls who lived, they told him, "in the best part of the city of Chicago on North Lake Shore Drive."

The girls argued incessantly about where they wished to go and Critchley adroitly concealed his ignorance of the places they visited by cramming in the guidebooks the night before. The only girl's name he could remember was "Denise" and in the ensuing years he had sometimes wondered what course their lives had taken, if they remembered their young, nervous guide, and if they still lived (perhaps married and with children) on North Lake Shore Drive.

On our final afternoon in London, anticipating a treasure to be renewed, I visited the British Museum. Moving from the sunlight of the courtyard into the shadows of that bountiful repository which receives almost 4 million visitors a year, I went directly to the galleries of Greek art. The statues of magnificent young athletes carved from marble and stone radiated the strength and grace the poet Pindar celebrated in his odes to the winners of the games. Yet the faces on the powerful bodies were reposeful, almost melancholy. As if the sculptors, capturing them in their triumph, also wished to convey the ephemerality of victories and the inevitability of their decline into age and death.

Approving that somber appraisal of human mortality, on a nearby pedestal loomed a great stone head of Zeus, the mightiest and most lascivious of Greek gods. Beneath majestic brows, his jeweled eyes pursued with carnality every female passing in his view.

I entered the Duveen gallery that held the marbles of the Parthenon. They had been taken from Greece to England in the nineteenth century by Lord Elgin, inciting a controversy about their possession and ownership that continues bitterly to this day. The present minister of culture in Greece, Melina Mercouri, demands they be returned where they belong. Aware of the sensitivity of the issue, a notice at the entrance of the gallery explains that Lord Elgin had only taken the marbles to save them from neglect, pilfering and wanton damage.

Whether their removal from Greece was grand theft or a desire to salvage great art, they were masterpieces. Among them were fifteen square panels or metopes portraying a battle between Centaurs and Lapiths. In legend the Centaurs were a wild tribe, half-human, half-horse, inhabiting the mountains of Thessaly. They were invited to the wedding feast of Peirithous, king of the human tribe of Lapithea, and, growing inflamed with wine, the lustful Centaurs attempted to abduct the bride and other women. Depicted in the panels, a savage battle ensued in which the Lapiths were victorious.

The stone gleams like crystal, manifesting energy and life. Every detail, whether a horse's tail, portions of reins, a hoof, or an ear is rendered in stunning detail. Grotesque and fierce, a Centaur in full gallop clutches a Lapith maiden, her face revealing terror and despair. On the ground lies a wounded Lapith warrior, his eyes starkly disclosing the shades of death. All the primal violence of passion, rage and violence leaps from the stone.

In contrast to the ferocity of that battle, the 247 feet of the Frieze from the Parthenon that hangs in the main gallery is ceremonial and tranquil, a procession depicting the presentation of the heroes of the battle of Marathon in 490 B.C. to the gods of Olympus. On either wall of the long gallery, in solemn, measured ritual, the horsemen of the cavalry lead the chariots, followed by the elders of the city, the musicians and gift-bearers, the priests and the sacrificial victims. A group of nymphs in flowing robes, guardians of streams, trees, and mountains, are flanked by a stately array of gods and goddesses. Every fold of cloth, strand of hair, curve of throat, line of lip and hollow of eye is vividly, exquisitely formed. The procession is majestic and eternal.

Resting on one of the benches, allowing my overpowered senses time to absorb the splendor of the panorama, I noticed that even the tourists around me seemed shaken. Moving noisily through other galleries, before the marbles their voices fell to whispers, their faces reflecting awe at witnessing that moment of glory created by artists more than two and a half thousand years ago.

Even if I hadn't been born in America of Greek parents, my spirit linked to my father and mother's homeland, justice decreed the Parthenon marbles should be returned to Greece. Their absence is a wound in the Greek soul. Yet a part of me understood that their presence in trust in the British Museum served a lofty purpose. That wasn't a betrayal of Greece but an awareness that millions of visitors from across the world would see them in the museum each year. Perhaps the marbles would stir in them, as they did in me at that moment, a longing to visit the small, often sorrowful, but inspiringly beautiful land from which the marbles began their journey.

A NOTE ON THE AUTHOR

Harry Mark Petrakis, who has lived most of his life in Chicago, is the author of seventeen books, including eight novels and four collections of short stories. His citations include two nominations for the National Book Award in fiction. Several of his novels and stories have been dramatized for film and television. He has been McGuffey Visiting Lecturer at Ohio University and has held the Kazantzakis Chair professorship at San Francisco State University. He has lectured widely and in the bardic tradition reads his stories before college and club audiences. He has three sons and four grandchildren and with his wife, Diana, now lives on the shores of Lake Michigan in Dune Acres, near the towns of Porter and Chesterton, Indiana.